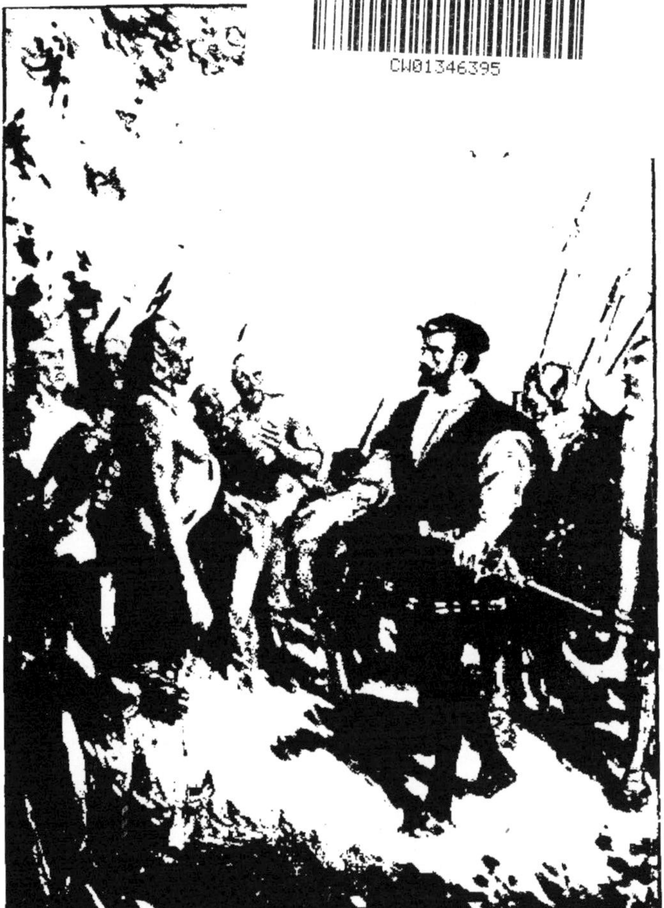

THE MARINER OF ST MALO

A Chronicle of the Voyages
of Jacques Cartier

BY

STEPHEN LEACOCK

TORONTO
GLASGOW, BROOK & COMPANY
1914

*Copyright in all Countries subscribing to
the Berne Convention*

CONTENTS

	Page
I. EARLY LIFE	1
II. THE FIRST VOYAGE—NEWFOUNDLAND AND LABRADOR	12
III. THE FIRST VOYAGE—THE GULF OF ST LAWRENCE	25
IV. THE SECOND VOYAGE—THE ST LAWRENCE	41
V. THE SECOND VOYAGE—STADACONA	53
VI. THE SECOND VOYAGE—HOCHELAGA	67
VII. THE SECOND VOYAGE—WINTER AT STADACONA	79
VIII. THE THIRD VOYAGE	93
IX. THE CLOSE OF CARTIER'S CAREER	105
ITINERARY OF CARTIER'S VOYAGES	113
BIBLIOGRAPHICAL NOTE	121
INDEX	123

ILLUSTRATIONS

JACQUES CARTIER AT HOCHELAGA, 1535 . *Frontispiece*
    From a colour-drawing by C. W. Jefferys.

JACQUES CARTIER . . . . . *Facing page* 2
    From the St Malo portrait.

JACQUES CARTIER . . . . . ,, 4
    From the medallion portrait in the National Library at Paris.

MAP OF CARTIER'S VOYAGES . . . ,, 16
    Prepared by James White, F.R.G.S.

THE 'GRANDE HERMINE,' 'PETITE HERMINE,' AND 'EMERILLON' IN THE ST LAWRENCE, 1535 . . . . ,, 54

CARTIER AT HOCHELAGA . . . ,, 70
    From a painting by Andrew Morris.

THE FINAL CEREMONY AT QUEBEC, MAY 3, 1536 . . . . . ,, 90
    From an old engraving.

CARTIER'S MANOR HOUSE AT LIMOILOU, NEAR ST MALO . . . . ,, 110
    From Baxter's 'Memoir of Jacques Cartier.'

CHAPTER I

EARLY LIFE

IN the town hall of the seaport of St Malo there hangs a portrait of Jacques Cartier, the great sea-captain of that place, whose name is associated for all time with the proud title of 'Discoverer of Canada.' The picture is that of a bearded man in the prime of life, standing on the deck of a ship, his bent elbow resting upon the gunwale, his chin supported by his hand, while his eyes gaze outward upon the western ocean as if seeking to penetrate its mysteries. The face is firm and strong, with tight-set jaw, prominent brow, and the full, inquiring eye of the man accustomed both to think and to act. The costume marks the sea-captain of four centuries ago. A thick cloak, gathered by a belt at the waist, enwraps the stalwart figure. On his head is the tufted Breton cap familiar in the pictures of the days of the great navigators. At the waist, on the left side, hangs a sword, and, on the right, close to the belt, the dirk or poniard of the period.

How like or unlike the features of Cartier this picture in the town hall may be, we have no means of telling. Painted probably in 1839, it has hung there for more than seventy years, and the record of the earlier prints or drawings from which its artist drew his inspiration no longer survives. We know, indeed, that an ancient map of the eastern coast of America, made some ten years after the first of Cartier's voyages, has pictured upon it a group of figures that represent the landing of the navigator and his followers among the Indians of Gaspé. It was the fashion of the time to attempt by such decorations to make maps vivid. Demons, deities, mythological figures and naked savages disported themselves along the borders of the maps and helped to decorate unexplored spaces of earth and ocean. Of this sort is the illustration on the map in question. But it is generally agreed that we have no right to identify Cartier with any of the figures in the scene, although the group as a whole undoubtedly typifies his landing upon the seacoast of Canada.

There is rumour, also, that the National Library at Paris contains an old print of

JACQUES CARTIER

From the St Malo Portrait

Cartier, who appears therein as a bearded man passing from the prime of life to its decline. The head is slightly bowed with the weight of years, and the face is wanting in that suggestion of unconquerable will which is the dominating feature of the portrait of St Malo. This is the picture that appears in the form of a medallion, or ring-shaped illustration, in more than one of the modern works upon the great adventurer. But here again we have no proofs of identity, for we know nothing of the origin of the portrait.

Curiously enough an accidental discovery of recent years seems to confirm in some degree the genuineness of the St Malo portrait. There stood until the autumn of 1908, in the French-Canadian fishing village of Cap-des-Rosiers, near the mouth of the St Lawrence, a house of very ancient date. Precisely how old it was no one could say, but it was said to be the oldest existing habitation of the settlement. Ravaged by perhaps two centuries of wind and weather, the old house afforded but little shelter against the boisterous gales and the bitter cold of the rude climate of the Gulf. Its owner decided to tear it down, and in doing so he stumbled upon a startling discovery. He found a dummy window that, generations before, had evidently been built over and concealed. From the cavity thus disclosed he drew forth a large wooden medallion, about twenty inches across, with the portrait of a man carved in relief. Here again are the tufted hat, the bearded face, and the features of the picture of St Malo. On the back of the wood, the deeply graven initials J. C. seemed to prove that the image which had lain hidden for generations behind the woodwork of the old Canadian house is indeed that of the great discoverer. Beside the initials is carved the date 1704. This wooden medallion would appear to have once figured as the stern shield of some French vessel, wrecked probably upon the Gaspé coast. As it must have been made long before the St Malo portrait was painted, the resemblance of the two faces perhaps indicates the existence of some definite and genuine portrait of Jacques Cartier, of which the record has been lost.

It appears, therefore, that we have the right to be content with the picture which hangs in the town hall of the seaport of St Malo. If it does not show us Cartier as he was,—and we have no absolute proof in the one or the other direction,—at least it shows us Cartier as he might well have been, with precisely the face

JACQUES CARTIER

From the medallion portrait in the National Library at Paris

EARLY LIFE 5

and bearing which the hero-worshipper would read into the character of such a discoverer.

The port of St Malo, the birthplace and the home of Cartier, is situated in the old province of Brittany, in the present department of Ille-et-Vilaine. It is thus near the lower end of the English Channel. To the north, about forty miles away, lies Jersey, the nearest of the Channel Islands, while on the west surges the restless tide of the broad Atlantic. The situation of the port has made it a nursery of hardy seamen. The town stands upon a little promontory that juts out as a peninsula into the ocean. The tide pours in and out of the harbour thus formed, and rises within the harbour to a height of thirty or forty feet. The rude gales of the western ocean spend themselves upon the rocky shores of this Breton coast. Here for centuries has dwelt a race of adventurous fishermen and navigators, whose daring is unsurpassed by any other seafaring people in the world.

The history, or at least the legend, of the town goes back ten centuries before the time of Cartier. It was founded, tradition tells us, by a certain Aaron, a pilgrim who landed there with his disciples in the year 507 A.D., and sought shelter upon the sea-girt promontory which has since borne the name of Aaron's Rock. Aaron founded a settlement. To the same place came, about twenty years later, a bishop of Castle Gwent, with a small band of followers. The leader of this flock was known as St Malo, and he gave his name to the seaport.

But the religious character of the first settlement soon passed away. St Malo became famous as the headquarters of the corsairs of the northern coast. These had succeeded the Vikings of an earlier day, and they showed a hardihood and a reckless daring equal to that of their predecessors. Later on, in more settled times, the place fell into the hands of the fishermen and traders of northern France. When hardy sailors pushed out into the Atlantic ocean to reach the distant shores of America, St Malo became a natural port and place of outfit for the passage of the western sea.

Jacques Cartier first saw the light in the year 1491. The family has been traced back to a grandfather who lived in the middle of the fifteenth century. This Jean Cartier, or Quartier, who was born in St Malo in 1428, took to wife in 1457 Guillemette Baudoin. Of the four sons that she bore him, Jamet, the eldest, married Geseline Jansart, and of their

EARLY LIFE

five children the second one, Jacques, rose to greatness as the discoverer of Canada. There is little to chronicle that is worth while of the later descendants of the original stock. Jacques Cartier himself was married in 1519 to Marie Katherine des Granches. Her father was the Chevalier Honoré des Granches, high constable of St Malo. In all probability he stood a few degrees higher in the social scale of the period than such plain seafaring folk as the Cartier family. From this, biographers have sought to prove that, early in life, young Jacques Cartier must have made himself a notable person among his townsmen. But the plain truth is that we know nothing of the circumstances that preceded the marriage, and have only the record of 1519 on the civil register of St Malo: 'The nuptial benediction was received by Jacques Cartier, master-pilot of the port of Saincte-Malo, son of Jamet Cartier and of Geseline Jansart, and Marie Katherine des Granches, daughter of Messire Honoré des Granches, chevalier of our lord the king, and constable of the town and city of Saint-Malo.'

Cartier's marriage was childless, so that he left no direct descendants. But the branches of the family descended from the original Jean Cartier appear on the registers of St Malo,

Saint Briac, and other places in some profusion during the sixteenth and seventeenth centuries. The family seems to have died out, although not many years ago direct descendants of Pierre Cartier, the uncle of Jacques, were still surviving in France.

It is perhaps no great loss to the world that we have so little knowledge of the ancestors and relatives of the famous mariner. It is, however, deeply to be deplored that, beyond the record of his voyages, we know so little of Jacques Cartier himself. We may take it for granted that he early became a sailor. Brought up at such a time and place, he could hardly have failed to do so. Within a few years after the great discovery of Columbus, the Channel ports of St Malo and Dieppe were sending forth adventurous fishermen to ply their trade among the fogs of the Great Banks of the New Land. The Breton boy, whom we may imagine wandering about the crowded wharves of the little harbour, must have heard strange tales from the sailors of the new discoveries. Doubtless he grew up, as did all the seafarers of his generation, with the expectation that at any time some fortunate adventurer might find behind the coasts and islands now revealed to Europe in the western

EARLY LIFE

sea the half-fabled empires of Cipango and Cathay. That, when a boy, he came into actual contact with sailors who had made the Atlantic voyage is not to be questioned. We know that in 1507 the *Pensée* of Dieppe had crossed to the coast of Newfoundland and that this adventure was soon followed by the sailing of other Norman ships for the same goal.

We have, however, no record of Cartier and his actual doings until we find his name in an entry on the baptismal register of St Malo. He stood as godfather to his nephew, Etienne Nouel, the son of his sister Jehanne. Strangely enough, this proved to be only the first of a great many sacred ceremonies of this sort in which he took part. There is a record of more than fifty baptisms at St Malo in the next forty-five years in which the illustrious mariner had some share; in twenty-seven of them he appeared as a godfather.

What voyages Cartier actually made before he suddenly appears in history as a pilot of the king of France and the protégé of the high admiral of France we do not know. This position in itself, and the fact that at the time of his marriage in 1519 he had already the rank of master-pilot, would show that he had made the Atlantic voyage. There is some faint evidence that he had even been to Brazil, for in the account of his first recorded voyage he makes a comparison between the maize of Canada and that of South America; and in those days this would scarcely have occurred to a writer who had not seen both plants of which he spoke. 'There groweth likewise,' so runs the quaint translation that appears in Hakluyt's *Voyages*, 'a kind of Millet as big as peason [*i.e.* peas] like unto that which groweth in Bresil.' And later on, in the account of his second voyage, he repeats the reference to Brazil; then 'goodly and large fields' which he saw on the present site of Montreal recall to him the millet fields of Brazil. It is possible, indeed, that not only had he been in Brazil, but that he had carried a native of that country to France. In a baptismal register of St Malo is recorded the christening, in 1528, of a certain 'Catherine of Brezil,' to whom Cartier's wife stood godmother. We may, in fancy at least, suppose that this forlorn little savage with the regal title was a little girl whom the navigator, after the fashion of his day, had brought home as living evidence of the existence of the strange lands that he had seen.

Out of this background, then, of uncertainty and conjecture emerges, in 1534, Jacques Cartier, a master-pilot in the prime of life, now sworn to the service of His Most Christian Majesty Francis I of France, and about to undertake on behalf of his illustrious master a voyage to the New Land.

CHAPTER II

THE FIRST VOYAGE—NEWFOUNDLAND AND LABRADOR

It was on April 20, 1534, that Jacques Cartier sailed out of the port of St Malo on his first voyage in the service of Francis I. Before leaving their anchorage the commander, the sailing-masters, and the men took an oath, administered by Charles de Mouy, vice-admiral of France, that they would behave themselves truly and faithfully in the service of the Most Christian King. The company were borne in two ships, each of about sixty tons burden, and numbered in all sixty-one souls.

The passage across the ocean was pleasant. Fair winds, blowing fresh and strong from the east, carried the clumsy caravels westward on the foaming crests of the Atlantic surges. Within twenty days of their departure the ice-bound shores of Newfoundland rose before their eyes. Straight in front of them was Cape Bonavista, the 'Cape of Happy Vision,' already

… known and named by the fishermen-explorers, who had welcomed the sight of its projecting headlands after the weary leagues of unbroken sea. But approach to the shore was impossible. The whole coastline was blocked with the 'great store of ice' that lay against it. The ships ran southward and took shelter in a little haven about five leagues south of the cape, to which Cartier gave the name St Catherine's Haven, either in fond remembrance of his wife, or, as is more probable, in recognition of the help and guidance of St Catherine, whose natal day, April 30, had fallen midway in his voyage. The harbourage is known to-day as Catalina, and lies distant, as the crow flies, about eighty miles north-westward of the present city of St John's in Newfoundland. Here the mariners remained ten days, 'looking for fair weather,' and engaged in mending and 'dressing' their boats.

At this time, it must be remembered, the coast of Newfoundland was, in some degree, already known. Ships had frequently passed through the narrow passage of Belle Isle that separates Newfoundland from the coast of Labrador. Of the waters, however, that seemed to open up beyond, or of the exact relation of the Newfoundland coastline to the rest of the great continent nothing accurate was known. It might well be that the inner waters behind the inhospitable headlands of Belle Isle would prove the gateway to the great empires of the East. Cartier's business at any rate was to explore, to see all that could be seen, and to bring news of it to his royal master. This he set himself to do, with the persevering thoroughness that was the secret of his final success. He coasted along the shore from cape to cape and from island to island, sounding and charting as he went, noting the shelter for ships that might be found, and laying down the bearing of the compass from point to point. It was his intent, good pilot as he was, that those who sailed after him should find it easy to sail on these coasts.

From St Catherine's Harbour the ships sailed on May 21 with a fine off-shore wind that made it easy to run on a course almost due north. As they advanced on this course the mainland sank again from sight, but presently they came to an island. It lay far out in the sea, and was surrounded by a great upheaval of jagged and broken ice. On it and around it they saw so dense a mass of birds that no one, declares Cartier, could have believed it who had not seen it for himself. The birds were as large as jays, they were coloured black and white, and they could scarcely fly because of their small wings and their exceeding fatness. The modern enquirer will recognize, perhaps, the great auk which once abounded on the coast, but which is now extinct. The sailors killed large numbers of the birds, and filled two boats with them. Then the ships sailed on rejoicing from the Island of Birds with six barrels full of salted provisions added to their stores. Cartier's Island of Birds is the Funk Island of our present maps.

The ships now headed west and north to come into touch with land again. To the great surprise of the company they presently met a huge polar bear swimming in the open sea, and evidently heading for the tempting shores of the Island of Birds. The bear was ' as great as any cow and as white as a swan.' The sailors lowered boats in pursuit, and captured 'by main force' the bear, which supplied a noble supper for the captors. ' Its flesh,' wrote Cartier, ' was as good to eat as any heifer of two years.'

The explorers sailed on westward, changing their course gradually to the north to follow the broad curve of the Atlantic coast of Newfoundland. Jutting headlands and outlying capes must have alternately appeared and disappeared on the western horizon. May 24 found the navigators off the entrance of Belle Isle. After four hundred years of maritime progress, the passage of the narrow strait that separates Newfoundland from Labrador remains still rough and dangerous, even for the great steel ships of to-day. We can imagine how forbidding it must have looked to Cartier and his companions from the decks of their small storm-tossed caravels. Heavy gales from the west came roaring through the strait. Great quantities of floating ice ground to and fro under the wind and current. So stormy was the outlook that for the time being the passage seemed impossible. But Cartier was not to be baulked in his design. He cast anchor at the eastern mouth of the strait, in what is now the little harbour of Kirpon (Carpunt), and there day after day, stormbound by the inclement weather, he waited until June 9. Then at last he was able to depart, hoping, as he wrote, 'with the help of God to sail farther.'

Having passed through the Strait of Belle Isle, Cartier crossed over to the northern coast. Two days of prosperous sailing with fair winds carried him far along the shore to a distance

NEWFOUNDLAND AND LABRADOR

of more than a hundred miles west of the entrance of the Strait of Belle Isle. Whether he actually touched on his way at the island now known as Belle Isle is a matter of doubt. He passed an island which he named St Catherine, and which he warned all mariners to avoid because of dangerous shoals that lay about it. We find his track again with certainty when he reaches the shelter of the Port of Castles. The name was given to the anchorage by reason of the striking cliffs of basaltic rock, which here give to the shore something of the appearance of a fortress. The place still bears the name of Castle Bay.

Sailing on to the west, Cartier noted the glittering expanse of Blanc Sablon (White Sands), still known by the name received from these first explorers. On June 10 the ships dropped anchor in the harbour of Brest, which lies on the northern coast of the Gulf of St Lawrence among many little islands lining the shore. This anchorage seems to have been known already in Cartier's time, and it became afterwards a famous place of gathering for the French fishermen. Later on in the sixteenth century a fort was erected there, and the winter settlement about it is said to have contained at one time as many as a thousand people. But its prosperity vanished later, and the fort had been abandoned before the great conflict had begun between France and Great Britain for the possession of North America. Cartier secured wood and water at Brest. Leaving his ships there for the time being, he continued his westward exploration in his boats.

The careful pilot marked every striking feature of the coast, the bearing of the headlands and the configuration of the many islands which stud these rock-bound and inhospitable shores. He spent a night on one of these islands, and the men found great quantities of ducks' eggs. The next day, still sailing to the west, he reached so fine an anchorage that he was induced to land and plant a cross there in honour of St Servan. Beyond this again was an island 'round like an oven.' Still farther on he found a great river, as he thought it, which came sweeping down from the highlands of the interior.

As the boats lay in the mouth of the river, there came bearing down upon them a great fishing ship which had sailed from the French port of La Rochelle, and was now seeking vainly for the anchorage of Brest. Cartier's careful observations now bore fruit. He and his men went in their small boats to the fishing ship and gave the information needed for the navigation of the coast. The explorers still pressed on towards the west, till they reached a place which Cartier declared to be one of the finest harbours of the world, and which he called Jacques Cartier Harbour. This is probably the water now known as Cumberland Harbour. The forbidding aspect of the northern shore and the adverse winds induced Cartier to direct his course again towards the south, to the mainland, as he thought, but really to the island of Newfoundland; and so he now turned back with his boats to rejoin the ships. The company gathered safely again at Brest on Sunday, June 14, and Cartier caused a mass to be sung.

During the week spent in exploring the north shore, Cartier had not been very favourably impressed by the country. It seemed barren and inhospitable. It should not, he thought, be called the New Land, but rather stones and wild crags and a place fit for wild beasts. The soil seemed worthless. 'In all the north land,' said he, 'I did not see a cart-load of good earth. To be short, I believe that this was the land that God allotted to Cain.' From time to time the explorers had caught sight of painted savages, with heads adorned with bright feathers and with bodies clad in the skins of wild beasts. They were roving upon the shore or passing in light boats made of bark among the island channels of the coast. 'They are men,' wrote Cartier, 'of an indifferent good stature and bigness, but wild and unruly. They wear their hair tied on the top like a wreath of hay and put a wooden pin within it, or any other such thing instead of a nail, and with them they bind certain birds' feathers. They are clothed with beasts' skins as well the men as women, but that the women go somewhat straighter and closer in their garments than the men do, with their waists girded. They paint themselves with certain roan colours. Their boats are made with the bark of birch trees, with the which they fish and take great store of seals, and, as far as we could understand since our coming thither, that is not their habitation, but they come from the mainland out of hotter countries to catch the said seals and other necessaries for their living.'

There has been much discussion as to these savages. It has been thought by some that they were a southern branch of the Eskimos, by others that they were Algonquin Indians who had wandered eastward from the St

NEWFOUNDLAND AND LABRADOR

Lawrence region. But the evidence goes to show that they belonged to the lost tribe of the 'Red Indians' of Newfoundland, the race which met its melancholy fate by deliberate and ruthless destruction at the hands of the whites. Cabot had already seen these people on his voyage to the coast, and described them as painted with 'red ochre.' Three of them he had captured and taken to England as an exhibit. For two hundred years after the English settlement of Newfoundland, these 'Red Indians' were hunted down till they were destroyed. 'It was considered meritorious,' says a historian of the island, 'to shoot a Red Indian. To "go to look for Indians" came to be as much a phrase as to "look for partridges." They were harassed from post to post, from island to island: their hunting and fishing stations were unscrupulously seized by the invading English. They were shot down without the least provocation, or captured to be exposed as curiosities to the rabble at fairs in the western towns of Christian England at twopence apiece.' So much for the ill-fated savages among whom Cartier planted his first cross.

On June 15, Cartier, disappointed, as we have seen, with the rugged country that he found on the northern shore, turned south again to pick up the mainland, as he called it, of Newfoundland. Sailing south from Brest to a distance of about sixty miles, he found himself on the same day off Point Rich on the west coast of Newfoundland, to which, from its appearance, he gave the name of the Double Cape. For three days the course lay to the south-west along the shore. The panorama that was unfolded to the eye of the explorer was cheerless. The wind blew cold and hard from the north-east. The weather was dark and gloomy, while through the rifts of the mist and fog that lay heavy on the face of the waters there appeared only a forbidding and scarcely habitable coast. Low lands with islands fringed the shore. Behind them great mountains, hacked and furrowed in their outline, offered an uninviting prospect. There was here no Eldorado such as, farther south, met the covetous gaze of a Cortez or a Pizarro, no land of promise luxuriant with the vegetation of the tropics such as had greeted the eyes of Columbus at his first vision of the Indies. A storm-bound coast, a relentless climate and a reluctant soil—these were the treasures of the New World as first known to the discoverer of Canada.

For a week Cartier and his men lay off the

NEWFOUNDLAND AND LABRADOR

coast. The headland of Cape Anguille marks the approximate southward limit of their exploration. Great gales drove the water in a swirl of milk-white foam among the rocks that line the foot of this promontory. Beyond this point they saw nothing of the Newfoundland shore, except that, as the little vessels vainly tried to beat their way to the south against the fierce storms, the explorers caught sight of a second great promontory that appeared before them through the mist. This headland Cartier called Cape St John. In spite of the difficulty of tracing the storm-set path of the navigators, it is commonly thought that the point may be identified as Cape Anguille, which lies about twenty-five miles north of Cape Ray, the southwest ' corner ' of Newfoundland.

Had Cartier been able to go forward in the direction that he had been following, he would have passed out between Newfoundland and Cape Breton island into the open Atlantic, and would have realized that his New Land was, after all, an island and not the mainland of the continent. But this discovery was reserved for his later voyage. He seems, indeed, when he presently came to the islands that lie in the mouth of the Gulf of St Lawrence, to have suspected that a passage here lay to the open sea. Doubtless the set of the wind and current revealed it to the trained instinct of the pilot. 'If it were so,' he wrote, 'it would be a great shortening as well of the time as of the way, if any perfection could be found in it.' But it was just as well that he did not seek further the opening into the Atlantic. By turning westward from the 'heel' of Newfoundland he was led to discover the milder waters and the more fortunate lands which awaited him on the further side of the Gulf.

CHAPTER III

THE FIRST VOYAGE—THE GULF OF ST LAWRENCE

On June 25 Cartier turned his course away from Newfoundland and sailed westward into what appeared to be open sea. But it was not long before he came in sight of land again. About sixty miles from the Newfoundland shore and thirty miles east from the Magdalen Islands, two abrupt rocks rise side by side from the sea; through one of them the beating surf has bored a passage, so that to Cartier's eye, as his ships hove in sight of them, the rocks appeared as three. At the present time a lighthouse of the Canadian government casts its rays from the top of one of these rocky islets, across the tossing waters of the Gulf. Innumerable sea-fowl encircled the isolated spot and built their nests so densely upon the rocks as to cover the whole of the upper surface. At the base of one of these Bird Rocks Cartier stopped his ships in their westward course, and his men killed great numbers of the birds so easily that he declared he could have filled thirty boats with them in an hour.

The explorers continued on their way, and a sail of a few hours brought them to an island like to none that they had yet seen. After the rock-bound coast of the north it seemed, indeed, a veritable paradise. Thick groves of splendid trees alternated with beautiful glades and meadow-land, while the fertile soil of the island, through its entire length of about six miles, was carpeted with bright flowers, blossoming peas, and the soft colours of the wild rose. 'One acre of this land,' said Cartier, ' is worth more than all the New Land.' The ships lay off the shore of the island all night and replenished the stores of wood and water. The land abounded with game; the men of St Malo saw bears and foxes, and, to their surprise they saw also great beasts that basked upon the shore, with ' two great teeth in their mouths like elephants.' One of these walruses,—for such they doubtless were,—was chased by the sailors, but cast itself into the sea and disappeared. We can imagine how, through the long twilight of the June evening, the lovely scene was loud with the voices

THE GULF OF ST LAWRENCE

of the exultant explorers. It was fitting that Cartier should name this island of good omen after his patron, the Seigneur de Brion, admiral of France. To this day the name Brion Island,—corrupted sometimes to Byron Island,—recalls the landing of Jacques Cartier.

From this temporary halting-place the ships sailed on down the west coast of the Magdalen Islands. The night of June 28 found them at anchor off Entry Island at the southern end of the group. From here a course laid to the south-west brought the explorers into sight of Prince Edward Island. This they supposed to be, of course, the mainland of the great American continent. Turning towards the north-west, the ships followed the outline of the coast. They sailed within easy sight of the shore, and from their decks the explorer and his companions were able to admire the luxuriant beauty of the scene. Here again was a land of delight: ' It is the fairest land,' wrote Cartier, ' that may possibly be seen, full of goodly meadows and trees.' All that it lacked was a suitable harbour, which the explorers sought in vain. At one point a shallow river ran rippling to the sea, and here they saw savages crossing the stream in their canoes, but they found no place where the ships could be brought to anchor.

July 1 found the vessels lying off the northern end of Prince Edward Island. Here they lowered the boats, and searched the shore-line for a suitable anchorage. As they rowed along a savage was seen running upon the beach and making signs. The boats were turned towards him, but, seized with a sudden panic, he ran away. Cartier landed a boat and set up a little staff in the sand with a woollen girdle and a knife, as a present for the fugitive and a mark of good-will.

It has been asserted that this landing on a point called Cap-des-Sauvages by Cartier, in memory of the incident, took place on the New Brunswick shore. But the weight of evidence is in favour of considering that North Cape in Prince Edward Island deserves the honour. As the event occurred on July 1, some writers have tried to find a fortunate coincidence in the landing of the discoverer of Canada on its soil on the day that became, three hundred and thirty-three years later, Dominion Day. But the coincidence is not striking. Cartier had already touched Canadian soil at Brest, which is at the extreme end of the Quebec coast, and on the Magdalen Islands.

THE GULF OF ST LAWRENCE

Cartier's boats explored the northern end of Prince Edward Island for many miles. All that he saw delighted him. 'We went that day on shore,' he wrote in his narrative, 'in four places, to see the goodly sweet and smelling trees that were there. We found them to be cedars, yews, pines, white elms, ash, willows, with many other sorts of trees to us unknown, but without any fruit. The grounds where no wood is are very fair, and all full of peason [peas], white and red gooseberries, strawberries, blackberries, and wild corn, even like unto rye, which seemed to have been sowed and ploughed. This country is of better temperature than any other land that can be seen, and very hot. There are many thrushes, stockdoves, and other birds. To be short, there wanteth nothing but good harbours.'

On July 2, the ships, sailing on westward from the head of Prince Edward Island, came in sight of the New Brunswick coast. They had thus crossed Northumberland Strait, which separates the island from the mainland. Cartier, however, supposed this to be merely a deep bay, extending inland on his left, and named it the Bay of St Lunario. Before him on the northern horizon was another headland, and to the left the deep triangular bay known now as Miramichi. The shallowness of the water and the low sunken aspect of the shore led him to decide, rightly, that there was to be found here no passage to the west. It was his hope, of course, that at some point on his path the shore might fold back and disclose to him the westward passage to the fabled empires of the East. The deep opening of the Chaleur Bay, which extended on the left hand as the ships proceeded north, looked like such an opening. Hopes ran high, and Cartier named the projecting horn which marks the southern side of the mouth of the bay the Cape of Good Hope. Like Vasco da Gama, when he rounded South Africa, Cartier now thought that he had found the gateway of a new world. The cheery name has, however, vanished from the map in favour of the less striking one of Point Miscou.

Cartier sailed across the broad mouth of the bay to a point on the north shore, now known as Port Daniel. Here his ships lay at anchor till July 12, in order that he might carry on, in boats, the exploration of the shore.

On July 6, after hearing mass, the first boat with an exploring party set forth and almost immediately fell in with a great number of savages coming in canoes from the southern shore. In all there were some forty or fifty canoes.

The Indians, as they leaped ashore, shouted and made signs to the French, and held up skins on sticks as if anxious to enter into trade. But Cartier was in no mind to run the risk of closer contact with so numerous a company of savages. The French would not approach the fleet of canoes, and the savages, seeing this, began to press in on the strangers. For a moment affairs looked threatening. Cartier's boat was surrounded by seven canoes filled with painted, gibbering savages. But the French had a formidable defence. A volley of musket shots fired by the sailors over the heads of the Indians dispersed the canoes in rapid flight. Finding, however, that no harm was done by the strange thunder of the weapons, the canoes came flocking back again, their occupants making a great noise and gesticulating wildly. They were, however, nervous, and when, as they came near, Cartier's men let off two muskets they were terrified; 'with great haste they began to flee, and would no more follow us.' But the next day after the boat had returned to the ships, the savages came near to the anchorage, and some parties landed and traded together. The Indians had with them furs which they offered gladly in exchange for the knives and iron tools given them by the sailors. Cartier presented them also with 'a red hat to give unto their captain.' The Indians seemed delighted with the exchange. They danced about on the shore, went through strange ceremonies in pantomime and threw seawater over their heads. 'They gave us,' wrote Cartier, 'whatsoever they had, not keeping anything, so that they were constrained to go back again naked, and made us signs that the next day they would come again and bring more skins with them.'

Four more days Cartier lingered in the bay. Again he sent boats from the ships in the hope of finding the westward passage, but to his great disappointment and grief the search was fruitless. The waters were evidently landlocked, and there was here, as he sadly chronicled, no thoroughfare to the westward sea. He met natives in large numbers. Hundreds of them —men, women, and children— came in their canoes to see the French explorers. They brought cooked meat, laid it on little pieces of wood, and, retreating a short distance, invited the French to eat. Their manner was as of those offering food to the gods who have descended from above. The women among them, coming fearlessly up to the explorers, stroked them with their hands, and then lifted these hands clasped to the sky, with every sign of joy and exultation. The Indians, as Cartier saw them, seemed to have no settled home, but to wander to and fro in their canoes, taking fish and game as they went. Their land appeared to him the fairest that could be seen, level as a pond; in every opening of the forest he saw wild grains and berries, roses and fragrant herbs. It was, indeed, a land of promise that lay basking in the sunshine of a Canadian summer. The warmth led Cartier to give to the bay the name it still bears—Chaleur.

On July 12 the ships went north again. Their progress was slow. Boisterous gales drove in great seas from the outer Gulf. At times the wind, blowing hard from the north, checked their advance and they had, as best they could, to ride out the storm. The sky was lowering and overcast, and thick mist and fog frequently enwrapped the ships. The 16th saw them driven by stress of weather into Gaspé Bay, where they lay until the 25th, with so dark a sky and so violent a storm raging over the Gulf that not even the daring seamen of St Malo thought it wise to venture out.

Here again they saw savages in great numbers, but belonging, so Cartier concluded, to a different tribe from those seen on the bay below. 'We gave them knives,' he wrote, 'combs, beads of glass, and other trifles of small value, for which they made many signs of gladness, lifting their hands up to heaven, dancing and singing in their boats.' They appeared to be a miserable people, in the lowest stage of savagery, going about practically naked, and owning nothing of any value except their boats and their fishing-nets. He noted that their heads were shaved except for a tuft 'on the top of the crown as long as a horse's tail.' This, of course, was the 'scalp lock,' so suggestive now of the horrors of Indian warfare, but meaning nothing to the explorer. From its presence it is supposed that the savages were Indians of the Huron-Iroquois tribe. Cartier thought, from their destitute state, that there could be no poorer people in the world.

Before leaving the Bay of Gaspé, Cartier planted a great wooden cross at the entrance of the harbour. The cross stood thirty feet high, and at the centre of it he hung a shield with three fleurs-de-lis. At the top was carved in ancient lettering the legend, 'VIVE LE ROY DE

FRANCE.' A large concourse of savages stood about the French explorers as they raised the cross to its place. 'So soon as it was up,' writes Cartier, 'we altogether kneeled down before them, with our hands towards heaven yielding God thanks: and we made signs unto them, shewing them the heavens, and that all our salvation depended only on Him which in them dwelleth; whereat they shewed a great admiration, looking first at one another and then at the cross.'

The little group of sailors kneeling about the cross newly reared upon the soil of Canada as a symbol of the Gospel of Christ and of the sovereignty of France, the wondering savages turning their faces in awe towards the summer sky, serene again after the passing storms,— all this formed an impressive picture, and one that appears and reappears in the literature of Canada. But the first effect of the ceremony was not fortunate. By a sound instinct the savages took fright; they rightly saw in the erection of the cross the advancing shadow of the rule of the white man. After the French had withdrawn to their ships, the chief of the Indians came out with his brother and his sons to make protest against what had been done. He made a long oration, which the French could not, of course, understand. Pointing shoreward to the cross and making signs, the chief gave it to be understood that the country belonged to him and his people. He and his followers were, however, easily pacified by a few gifts and with the explanation, conveyed by signs, that the cross was erected to mark the entrance of the bay. The French entertained their guests bountifully with food and drink, and, having gaily decked out two sons of the chief in French shirts and red caps, they invited these young savages to remain on the ship and to sail with Cartier. They did so, and the chief and the others departed rejoicing. The next day the ships weighed anchor, surrounded by boat-loads of savages who shouted and gesticulated their farewells to those on board.

Cartier now turned his ships to the northeast. Westward on his left hand, had he known it, was the opening of the St Lawrence. From the trend of the land he supposed, however, that, by sailing in an easterly direction, he was again crossing one of the great bays of the coast. This conjecture seemed to be correct, as the coastline of the island of Anticosti presently appeared on the horizon. From July 27 until August 5 the explorers made their way along the shores of Anticosti, which they almost circumnavigated. Sailing first to the east they passed a low-lying country, almost bare of forests, but with verdant and inviting meadows. The shore ended at East Cape, named by Cartier Cape St Louis, and at this point the ships turned and made their way north-westward, along the upper shore of the island. On August 1, as they advanced, they came in sight of the mainland of the northern shore of the Gulf of St Lawrence, a low, flat country, heavily wooded, with great mountains forming a jagged sky-line. Cartier had now, evidently enough, come back again to the side of the great Gulf from which he had started, but, judging rightly that the way to the west might lie beyond the Anticosti coast, he continued on his voyage along that shore. Yet with every day progress became more difficult. As the ships approached the narrower waters between the west end of Anticosti and the mainland they met powerful tides and baffling currents. The wind, too, had turned against them and blew fiercely from the west.

For five days the intrepid mariners fought against the storms and currents that checked their advance. They were already in sight of what seemed after long searching to be the opening of the westward passage. But the fierce wind from the west so beat against them that the clumsy vessels could make no progress against it. Cartier lowered a boat, and during two hours the men rowed desperately into the wind. For a while the tide favoured them, but even then it ran so hard as to upset one of the boats. When the tide turned matters grew worse. There came rushing down with the wind and the current of the St Lawrence such a turmoil of the waters that the united strength of the thirteen men at the oars could not advance the boats by a stone's-throw. The whole company landed on the island of Anticosti, and Cartier, with ten or twelve men, made his way on foot to the west end. Standing there and looking westward over the foaming waters lashed by the August storm, he was able to realize that the goal of his search for the coast of Asia, or at least for an open passage to the west, might lie before him, but that, for the time being, it was beyond his reach.

Turning back, the party rejoined the ships which had drifted helplessly before the wind some twelve miles down the shore. Arrived on board, Cartier called together his sailing-master, pilots, and mates to discuss what was to be done. They agreed that the contrary winds forbade further exploration. The season was already late; the coast of France was far away; within a few weeks the great gales of the equinox would be upon them. Accordingly the company decided to turn back. Soon the ships were heading along the northern shore of the Gulf, and with the boisterous wind behind them were running rapidly towards the east. They sailed towards the Newfoundland shore, caught sight of the Double Cape and then, heading north again, came to Blanc Sablon on August 9. Here they lay for a few days to prepare for the homeward voyage, and on August 15 they were under way once more for the passage of Belle Isle and the open sea.

'And after that, upon August 15,' so ends Cartier's narrative, 'being the feast of the Assumption of our Lady, after that we had heard service, we altogether departed from the port of Blanc Sablon, and with a happy and prosperous weather we came into the middle of the sea that is between Newfoundland and Brittany, in which place we were tossed and turmoiled three days long with great storms and windy tempests coming from the east, which with the aid and assistance of God we suffered: then had we fair weather, and upon the fifth of September, in the said year, we came to the port of St Malo whence we departed.'

CHAPTER IV

THE SECOND VOYAGE—THE ST LAWRENCE

The second voyage of Jacques Cartier, undertaken in the years 1535 and 1536, is the exploit on which his title to fame chiefly rests. In this voyage he discovered the river St Lawrence, visited the site of the present city of Quebec, and, ascending the river as far as Hochelaga, was enabled to view from the summit of Mount Royal the imposing panorama of plain and river and mountain which marks the junction of the St Lawrence and the Ottawa. He brought back to the king of France the rumour of great countries still to be discovered to the west, of vast lakes and rivers reaching so far inland that no man could say from what source they sprang, and the legend of a region rich with gold and silver that should rival the territory laid at the feet of Spain by the conquests of Cortez. If he did not find the long-sought passage to the Western Sea, at least he added to the dominions of France a territory the potential wealth of which, as we now see, was not surpassed even by the riches of Cathay.

The report of Cartier's first voyage, written by himself, brought to him the immediate favour of the king. A commission, issued under the seal of Philippe Chabot, admiral of France, on October 30, 1534, granted to him wide powers for employing ships and men, and for the further prosecution of his discoveries. He was entitled to engage at the king's charge three ships, equipped and provisioned for fifteen months, so that he might be able to spend, at least, an entire year in actual exploration. Cartier spent the winter in making his preparations, and in the springtime of the next year (1535) all was ready for the voyage.

By the middle of May the ships, duly manned and provisioned, lay at anchor in the harbour of St Malo, waiting only a fair wind to sail. They were three in number—the *Grande Hermine* of 120 tons burden; a ship of 60 tons which was rechristened the *Petite Hermine*, and which was destined to leave its timbers in the bed of a little rivulet beside Quebec, and a small vessel of 40 tons known as the *Emerillon* or *Sparrow Hawk*. On the largest of the ships Cartier himself sailed, with Claude

THE ST LAWRENCE

de Pont Briand, Charles de la Pommeraye, and other gentlemen of France, lured now by a spirit of adventure to voyage to the New World. Mace Jalobert, who had married the sister of Cartier's wife, commanded the second ship. Of the sailors the greater part were trained seamen of St Malo. Seventy-four of their names are still preserved upon a roll of the crew. The company numbered in all one hundred and twelve persons, including the two savages who had been brought from Gaspé in the preceding voyage, and who were now to return as guides and interpreters of the expedition.

Whether or not there were any priests on board the ships is a matter that is not clear. The titles of two persons in the roll—Dom Guillaume and Dom Antoine—seem to suggest a priestly calling. But the fact that Cartier made no attempt to baptize the Indians to whom he narrated the truths of the Gospel, and that he makes no mention of priests in connection with any of the sacred ceremonies which he carried out, seem to show that none were included in the expedition. There is, indeed, reference in the narrative to the hearing of mass, but it relates probably to the mere reading of prayers by the explorer himself. On one occasion, also, as will appear,

Cartier spoke to the Indians of what his priests had told him, but the meaning of the phrase is doubtful.

Before sailing, every man of the company repaired to the Cathedral Church of St Malo, where all confessed their sins and received the benediction of the good bishop of the town. This was on the day and feast of Pentecost in 1535, and three days later, on May 19, the ships sailed out from the little harbour and were borne with a fair wind beyond the horizon of the west. But the voyage was by no means as prosperous as that of the year before. The ships kept happily together until May 26. Then they were assailed in mid-Atlantic by furious gales from the west, and were enveloped in dense banks of fog. During a month of buffeting against adverse seas, they were driven apart and lost sight of one another.

Cartier in the *Grande Hermine* reached the coast of Newfoundland safely on July 7, coming again to the Island of Birds. 'So full of birds it was,' he writes, 'that all the ships of France might be loaded with them, and yet it would not seem that any were taken away.' On the next day the *Grande Hermine* sailed on through the Strait of Belle Isle for Blanc Sablon, and there, by agreement, waited in the hope that her consorts might arrive. In the end, on the 26th, the two missing ships sailed into the harbour together. Three days more were spent in making necessary repairs and in obtaining water and other supplies, and on the 29th at sunrise the reunited expedition set out on its exploration of the northern shore. During the first half of August their way lay over the course already traversed from the Strait of Belle Isle to the western end of Anticosti. The voyage along this coast was marked by no event of especial interest. Cartier, as before, noted carefully the bearing of the land as he went along, took soundings, and, in the interest of future pilots of the coast, named and described the chief headlands and landmarks as he passed. He found the coast for the most part dangerous and full of shoals. Here and there vast forests extended to the shore, but otherwise the country seemed barren and uninviting.

From the north shore Cartier sailed across to Anticosti, touching near what is now called Charleton Point; but, meeting with head winds, which, as in the preceding year, hindered his progress along the island, he turned to the north again and took shelter in what he called a 'goodly great gulf full of islands, passages, and entrances towards what wind soever you please to bend.' It might be recognized, he said, by a great island that runs out beyond the rest and on which is 'an hill fashioned as it were an heap of corn.' The 'goodly gulf' is Pillage Bay in the district of Saguenay, and the hill is Mount Ste Geneviève.

From this point the ships sailed again to Anticosti and reached the extreme western cape of that island. The two Indian guides were now in a familiar country. The land in sight, they told Cartier, was a great island; south of it was Gaspé, from which country Cartier had taken them in the preceding summer; two days' journey beyond the island towards the west lay the kingdom of Saguenay, a part of the northern coast that stretches westwards towards the land of Canada. The use of this name, destined to mean so much to later generations, here appears for the first time in Cartier's narrative. The word was evidently taken from the lips of the savages, but its exact significance has remained a matter of dispute. The most fantastic derivations have been suggested. Charlevoix, writing two hundred years later, even tells us that the name originated from the fact that the Spaniards had been upon the coast before Cartier, looking for mines. Their search proving fruitless, they kept repeating *aca nada* (that is 'nothing here') in the hearing of the savages, who repeated the words to the French, thus causing them to suppose this to be the name of the country. There seems no doubt, however, that the word is Indian, though whether it is from the Iroquois Kannata, a settlement, or from some term meaning a narrow strait or passage, it is impossible to say.

From Anticosti, which Cartier named the Island of the Assumption, the ships sailed across to the Gaspé side of the Gulf, which they saw on August 16, and which was noted to be a land 'full of very great and high hills.' According to the information of his Indian guides, he had now reached the point beyond which extended the great kingdom of Saguenay. The northern and southern coasts were evidently drawing more closely together, and between them, so the savages averred, lay a great river.

'There is,' wrote Cartier in his narrative, 'between the southerly lands and the northerly about thirty leagues distance and more than two hundred fathoms depth. The said men did, moreover, certify unto us that there was the way and beginning of the great river of Hochelaga, and ready way to Canada, which river the farther it went the narrower it came, even unto Canada, and that then there was fresh water which went so far upwards that they had never heard of any man who had gone to the head of it, and that there is no other passage but with small boats.'

The announcement that the waters in which he was sailing led inward to a fresh-water river brought to Cartier not the sense of elation that should have accompanied so great a discovery, but a feeling of disappointment. A fresh-water river could not be the westward passage to Asia that he had hoped to find, and, interested though he might be in the rumoured kingdom of Saguenay, it was with reluctance that he turned from the waters of the Gulf to the ascent of the great river. Indeed, he decided not to do this until he had tried by every means to find the wished-for opening on the coast of the Gulf. Accordingly, he sailed to the northern shore and came to the land among the Seven Islands, which lie near the mouth of the Ste Marguerite river, about eighty-five miles west of Anticosti,—the Round Islands, Cartier called them. Here, having brought the ships to a safe anchorage, riding in twenty fathoms of water, he sent the boats eastward to explore the portion of the coast towards Anticosti which he had not yet seen. He cherished a last hope that here, perhaps, the westward passage might open before him. But the boats returned from the expedition with no news other than that of a river flowing into the Gulf, in such volume that its water was still fresh three miles from the shore. The men declared, too, that they had seen 'fishes shaped like horses,' which, so the Indians said, retired to shore at night, and spent the day in the sea. The creatures, no doubt, were walruses.

It was on August 15 that Cartier had left Anticosti for the Gaspé shore: it was not until the 24th that, delayed by the exploring expeditions of the boats and by heavy fogs and contrary winds, he moved out from the anchorage at the Seven Islands to ascend the St Lawrence. The season was now far advanced. By this time, doubtless, Cartier had realized that the voyage would not result in the discovery of the passage to the East. But, anxious not to return home without having some success to report, he was in any case prepared to winter in the New Land. Even though he did not find the passage, it was better to remain long enough to explore the lands in the basin of the great river than to return home without adding anything to the exploits of the previous voyage.

The expedition moved westward up the St Lawrence, the first week's sail bringing them as far as the Saguenay. On the way Cartier put in at Bic Islands, and christened them in honour of St John. Finding here but scanty shelter and a poor anchorage, he went on without further delay to the Saguenay, the mouth of which he reached on September 1. Here this great tributary river, fed from the streams and springs of the distant north, pours its mighty waters between majestic cliffs into the St Lawrence—truly an impressive sight. So vast is the flood that the great stream in its wider reaches shows a breadth of three miles, and in places the waters are charted as being more than eight hundred and seventy feet deep. Narrowing at its mouth, it enters the St Lawrence in an angry flood, shortly after passing the vast and frowning rocks of Cape Eternity and Cape Trinity, rising to a height of fifteen hundred feet. High up on the face of the cliffs, Cartier saw growing huge pine-trees that clung, earthless, to the naked

THE ST LAWRENCE 51

rock. Four canoes danced in the foaming water at the river mouth: one of them made bold to approach the ships, and the words of Cartier's Indian interpreters so encouraged its occupants that they came on board. The canoes, so these Indians explained to Cartier, had come down from Canada to fish.

Cartier did not remain long at the Saguenay. On the next day, September 2, the ships resumed their ascent of the St Lawrence. The navigation at this point was by no means easy. The river here feels the full force of the tide, whose current twists and eddies among the great rocks that lie near the surface of the water. The ships lay at anchor that night off Hare Island. As they left their moorings, at dawn of the following day, they fell in with a great school of white whales disporting themselves in the river. Strange fish, indeed, these seemed to Cartier. 'They were headed like greyhounds,' he wrote, 'and were as white as snow, and were never before of any man seen or known.'

Four days more brought the voyagers to an island, a 'goodly and fertile spot covered with fine trees,' and among them so many filbert-trees that Cartier gave it the name Isle-aux-Coudres (the Isle of Filberts), which it still bears. On September 7 the vessels sailed about thirty miles beyond Isle-aux-Coudres, and came to a group of islands, one of which, extending for about twenty miles up the river, appeared so fertile and so densely covered with wild grapes hanging to the river's edge, that Cartier named it the Isle of Bacchus. He himself, however, afterwards altered the name to the Island of Orleans. These islands, so the savages said, marked the beginning of the country known as Canada.

CHAPTER V

THE SECOND VOYAGE—STADACONA

At the time when Cartier ascended the St Lawrence, a great settlement of the Huron-Iroquois Indians existed at Quebec. Their village was situated below the heights, close to the banks of the St Charles, a small tributary of the St Lawrence. Here the lodges of the tribe gave shelter to many hundred people. Beautiful trees—elm and ash and maple and birch, as fair as the trees of France—adorned the banks of the river, and the open spaces of the woods waved with the luxuriant growth of Indian corn. Here were the winter home of the tribe and the wigwam of the chief. From this spot hunting and fishing parties of the savages descended the great river and wandered as far as the pleasant country of Chaleur Bay. Sixty-four years later, when Champlain ascended the St Lawrence, the settlement and the tribe that formerly occupied the spot had vanished. But in the time of Cartier the Quebec village, under its native name of Stadacona, seems to have been, next to Hochelaga, the most important lodgment of the Huron-Iroquois Indians of the St Lawrence valley.

As the French navigators wandered on the shores of the Island of Orleans, they fell in with a party of the Stadacona Indians. These, frightened at the strange faces and unwonted dress of the French, would have taken to flight, but Cartier's two Indians, whose names are recorded as Taignoagny and Domagaya, called after them in their own language. Great was the surprise of the natives not only to hear their own speech, but also to recognize in Taignoagny and Domagaya two members of their own tribe. The two guides, so far as we can judge from Cartier's narrative, had come down from the Huron-Iroquois settlements on the St Lawrence to the Gaspé country, whence Cartier had carried them to France. Their friends now surrounded them with tumultuous expressions of joy, leaping and shouting as if to perform a ceremonial of welcome. Without fear now of the French they followed them down to their boats, and brought them a plentiful supply of corn and of the great pumpkins that were ripening in their fields.

The *GRANDE HERMINE*, *PETITE HERMINE*, and *EMERILLON*

STADACONA

The news of the arrival of the strangers spread at once through the settlement. To see the ships, canoe after canoe came floating down the river. They were filled with men and women eager to welcome their returned kinsmen and to share in the trinkets which Cartier distributed with a liberal hand. On the next day the chief of the tribe, the lord of Canada, as Cartier calls him, Donnacona by name, visited the French ships. The ceremonial was appropriate to his rank. Twelve canoes filled with Indian warriors appeared upon the stream. As they neared the ships, at a command from Donnacona, all fell back except two, which came close alongside the *Emerillon*. Donnacona then delivered a powerful and lengthy harangue, accompanied by wondrous gesticulations of body and limbs. The canoes then moved down to the side of the *Grande Hermine*, where Donnacona spoke with Cartier's guides. As these savages told him of the wonders they had seen in France, he was apparently moved to very transports of joy. Nothing would satisfy him but that Cartier should step down into the canoe, that the chief might put his arms about his neck in sign of welcome. Cartier, unable to rival Donnacona's oratory, made up for it by causing the sailors hand down food and wine, to the keen delight of the Indians. This being done, the visitors departed with every expression of good-will.

Waiting only for a favourable tide, the ships left their anchorage, and, sailing past the Island of Orleans, cast anchor in the St Charles river, where it flows into the St Lawrence near Quebec. The *Emerillon* was left at anchor out in the St Lawrence, in readiness for the continuance of the journey, but the two larger vessels were moored at the point where a rivulet, the Lairet, runs into the St Charles. It was on the left bank of the Lairet that Cartier's fort was presently constructed for his winter occupancy. Some distance across from it, on the other side of the St Charles, was Stadaçona itself. Its site cannot be determined with exactitude, but it is generally agreed that it was most likely situated in the space between the present Rue de la Fabrique and the Côte Sainte-Geneviève.

The Indians were most friendly. When, on September 14, the French had sailed into the St Charles, Donnacona had again met them, accompanied by twenty-five canoes filled with his followers. The savages, by their noisy conduct and strange antics, gave every sign of joy over the arrival of the French. But from the first Cartier seems to have had his misgivings as to their good faith. He was struck by the fact that his two Indian interpreters, who had rejoined the ranks of their countrymen, seemed now to receive him with a sullen distrust, and refused his repeated invitations to re-enter his ships. He asked them whether they were still willing to go on with him to Hochelaga, of which they had told him, and which it was his purpose to visit. The two Indians assented, but their manner was equivocal and inspired Cartier with distrust.

The day after this a great concourse of Indians came again to the river bank to see the strangers, but Donnacona and his immediate followers, including Taignoagny and Domagaya, stood apart under a point of land on the river bank sullenly watching the movements of the French, who were busied in setting out buoys and harbour-marks for their anchorage. Cartier, noticing this, took a few of his sailors, fully armed, and marched straight to where the chief stood. Taignoagny, the interpreter, came forward and entered upon a voluble harangue, telling the French captain that Donnacona was grieved to see him and his men so fully armed, while he and his people bore no weapons in their hands. Cartier told Taignoagny, who had been in France, that to carry arms was the custom of his country, and that he knew it. Indeed, since Donnacona continued to make gestures of pleasure and friendship, the explorer concluded that the interpreter only and not the Indian chief was the cause of the distrust. Yet he narrates that before Donnacona left them, 'all his people at once with a loud voice cast out three great cries, a horrible thing to hear.' The Indian war-whoop, if such it was, is certainly not a reassuring sound, but Cartier and Donnacona took leave of one another with repeated assurances of good-will.

The following day, September 16, the Indians came again. About five hundred of them, so Cartier tells us, gathered about the ships. Donnacona, with 'ten or twelve of the chiefest men of the country,' came on board the ships, where Cartier held a great feast for them and gave them presents in accordance with their rank. Taignoagny explained to Cartier that Donnacona was grieved that he was going up to Hochelaga. The river, said the guide, was of no importance, and the journey was not worth while. Cartier's reply to this protest was that he had been commanded by his king to go as far as he could go, but that, after seeing Hochelaga, he would come back again. On this Taignoagny flatly refused to act as guide, and the Indians abruptly left the ship and went ashore.

Cartier must, indeed, have been perplexed, and perhaps alarmed, at the conduct of the Stadacona natives. It was his policy throughout his voyages to deal with the Indians fairly and generously, to avoid all violence towards them, and to content himself with bringing to them the news of the Gospel and the visible signs of the greatness of the king of France. The cruelties of the Spanish conquerors of the south were foreign to his nature. The few acts of injustice with which his memory has been charged may easily be excused in the light of the circumstances of his age. But he could not have failed to realize the possibilities of a sudden and murderous onslaught on the part of savages who thus combined a greedy readiness for feasting and presents with a sullen and brooding distrust.

Donnacona and his people were back again on the morrow, still vainly endeavouring to dissuade the French from their enterprise. They brought with them a great quantity of eels and fish as presents, and danced and sang upon the shore opposite the ships in token of their friendship. When Cartier and his men came ashore, Donnacona made all his people stand back from the beach. He drew in the sand a huge ring, and into this he led the French. Then, selecting from the ranks of his followers, who stood in a great circle watching the ceremony, a little girl of ten years old, he led her into the ring and presented her to Cartier. After her, two little boys were handed over in the same fashion, the assembled Indians rending the air with shouts of exultation. Donnacona, in true Indian fashion, improved the occasion with a long harangue, which Taignoagny interpreted to mean that the little girl was the niece of the chief and one of the boys the brother of the interpreter himself, and that the explorer might keep all these children as a gift if he would promise not to go to Hochelaga.

Cartier at once, by signs and speech, offered the children back again, whereupon the other interpreter, Domagaya, broke in and said that the children were given in good-will, and that Donnacona was well content that Cartier should go to Hochelaga. The three poor little savages were carried to the boats, the two interpreters wrangling and fighting the while as to what had really been said. But Cartier felt assured that the treachery, if any were contemplated, came only from one of them, Taignoagny. As a great mark of trust he gave to Donnacona two swords, a basin of plain brass and a ewer—gifts which called forth renewed shouts of joy. Before the assemblage broke up, the chief asked Cartier to cause the ships' cannons to be fired, as he had learned from the two guides that they made such a marvellous noise as was never heard before.

'Our captain answered,' writes Cartier in his narrative, ' that he was content: and by and by he commanded his men to shoot off twelve cannons into the wood that was hard by the people and the ships, at which noise they were greatly astonished and amazed, for they thought the heaven had fallen upon them, and put themselves to flight, howling, crying and shrieking, so that it seemed hell was broken loose.'

Next day the Indians made one more attempt to dissuade Cartier from his journey. Finding that persuasion and oratory were of no avail, they decided to fall back upon the supernatural and to frighten the French from their design.

Their artifice was transparent enough, but to the minds of the simple savages was calculated to strike awe into the hearts of their visitors. Instead of coming near the ships, as they had done on each preceding day, the Indians secreted themselves in the woods along the shore. There they lay hid for many hours, while the French were busied with their preparations for departure. But later in the day, when the tide was running swiftly outward, the Indians in their canoes came paddling down the stream towards the ships, not, however, trying to approach them, but keeping some little distance away as if in expectation of something unusual.

The mystery soon revealed itself. From beneath the foliage of the river bank a canoe shot into the stream, the hideous appearance of its occupants contrasting with the bright autumn tints that were lending their glory to the Canadian woods. The three Indians in the canoe had been carefully made up by their fellows as ' stage devils ' to strike horror into Cartier and his companions. They were ' dressed like devils, being wrapped in dog skins, white and black, their faces besmeared as black as any coals, with horns on their heads more than a yard long.' The canoe came

STADACONA

rushing swiftly down the stream, and floated past the ships, the 'devils' who occupied the craft making no attempt to stop, not even turning towards the ships, but counterfeiting, as it were, the sacred frenzy of angry deities. The devil in the centre shouted a fierce harangue into the air. No sooner did the canoe pass the ships than Donnacona and his braves in their light barques set after it, paddling so swiftly as to overtake the canoe of the 'devils' and seize the gunwale of it in their hands.

The whole thing was a piece of characteristic Indian acting, viewed by the French with interest, but apparently without the faintest alarm. The 'devils,' as soon as their boat was seized by the profane touch of the savages, fell back as if lifeless in their canoe. The assembled flotilla was directed to the shore. The 'devils' were lifted out rigid and lifeless and carried solemnly into the forest. The leaves of the underbrush closed behind them and they were concealed from sight, but from the deck of the ship the French could still hear the noise of cries and incantations that broke the stillness of the woods. After half an hour Taignoagny and Domagaya issued from among the trees. Their walk and their actions were solemnity itself, while their faces simulated the religious ecstasy of men who have spoken with the gods. The caps that they had worn were now placed beneath the folds of their Indian blankets, and their clasped hands were uplifted to the autumn sky. Taignoagny cried out three times upon the name of Jesus, while his fellow imitated and kept shouting, 'Jesus! the Virgin Mary! Jacques Cartier!'

Cartier very naturally called to them to know what was the matter; whereupon Taignoagny in doleful tones called out, 'Ill news!' Cartier urged the Indian to explain, and the guide, still acting the part of one who bears tidings from heaven, said that the great god, Cudragny, had spoken at Hochelaga and had sent down three 'spirits' in the canoe to warn Cartier that he must not try to come to Hochelaga, because there was so much ice and snow in that country that whoever went there should die. In the face of this awful revelation, Cartier showed a cheerful and contemptuous scepticism. 'Their god, Cudragny,' he said, must be 'a fool and a noodle,' and that, as for the cold, Christ would protect his followers from that, if they would but believe in Him. Taignoagny asked Cartier if he had spoken with Jesus. Cartier answered no, but said that his priests had done so and that Jesus had told them that the weather would be fine. Taignoagny, hypocrite still, professed a great joy at hearing this, and set off into the woods, whence he emerged presently with the whole band of Indians, singing and dancing. Their plan had failed, but they evidently thought it wiser to offer no further opposition to Cartier's journey, though all refused to go with him.

The strange conduct of Donnacona and his Indians is not easy to explain. It is quite possible that they meditated some treachery towards the French: indeed, Cartier from first to last was suspicious of their intentions, and, as we shall see, was careful after his return to Stadacona never to put himself within their power. To the very end of his voyage he seems to have been of the opinion that if he and his men were caught off their guard, Donnacona and his braves would destroy the whole of them for the sake of their coveted possessions. The stories that he heard now and later from his guides of the horrors of Indian war and of a great massacre at the Bic Islands certainly gave him just grounds for suspicion and counselled prudence. Some writers are agreed, however, that the Indians had no hostile intentions whatever. The new-comers seemed to them wondrous beings, floating on the surface of the water in great winged houses, causing the thunder to roll forth from their abode at will and, more than all, feasting their friends and giving to them such gifts as could only come from heaven. Such guests were too valuable to lose. The Indians knew well of the settlement at Hochelaga, and of the fair country where it lay. They feared that if Cartier once sailed to it, he and his presents—the red caps and the brass bowls sent direct from heaven—would be lost to them for ever.

Be this as it may, no further opposition was offered to the departure of the French. The two larger ships, with a part of the company as guard, were left at their moorings. Cartier in the *Emerillon*, with Mace Jalobert, Claude de Pont Briand, and the other gentlemen of the expedition, a company of fifty in all, set out for Hochelaga.

CHAPTER VI

THE SECOND VOYAGE—HOCHELAGA

NINE days of prosperous sailing carried Cartier in his pinnace from Stadacona to the broad expansion of the St Lawrence, afterwards named Lake St Peter. The autumn scene as the little vessel ascended the stream was one of extreme beauty. The banks of the river were covered with glorious forests resplendent now with the red and gold of the turning leaves. Grape-vines grew thickly on every hand, laden with their clustered fruit. The shore and forest abounded with animal life. The woods were loud with the chirruping of thrushes, goldfinches, canaries, and other birds. Countless flocks of wild geese and ducks passed overhead, while from the marshes of the back waters great cranes rose in their heavy flight over the bright surface of the river that reflected the cloudless blue of the autumn sky.

Cartier was enraptured with the land which he had discovered,—' as goodly a country,' he wrote, 'as possibly can with eye be seen, and all replenished with very goodly trees.' Here and there the wigwams of the savages dotted the openings of the forest. Often the inhabitants put off from shore in canoes, bringing fish and food, and accepting, with every sign of friendship, the little presents which Cartier distributed among them. At one place an Indian chief—' one of the chief lords of the country,' says Cartier—brought two of his children as a gift to the miraculous strangers. One of the children, a little girl of eight, was kept upon the ship and went on with Cartier to Hochelaga and back to Stadacona, where her parents came to see her later on. The other child Cartier refused to keep because ' it was too young, for it was but two or three years old.'

At the head of Lake St Peter, Cartier, ignorant of the channels, found his progress in the pinnace barred by the sand bars and shallows among the group of islands which here break the flow of the great river. The Indians whom he met told him by signs that Hochelaga lay still farther up-stream, at a distance of three days' journey. Cartier decided to leave the *Emerillon* and to continue on his way in the two boats which he had brought with him. Claude de Pont Briand and some of the gentlemen, together with twenty mariners, accompanied the leader, while the others remained in charge of the pinnace.

Three days of easy and prosperous navigation was sufficient for the journey, and on October 2, Cartier's boats, having rowed along the shores of Montreal island, landed in full sight of Mount Royal, at some point about three or four miles from the heart of the present city. The precise location of the landing has been lost to history. It has been thought by some that the boats advanced until the foaming waters of the Lachine rapids forbade all further progress. Others have it that the boats were halted at the foot of St Mary's current, and others again that Nun Island was the probable place of landing. What is certain is that the French brought their boats to shore among a great crowd of assembled savages,—a thousand persons, Cartier says,—and that they were received with tumultuous joy. The Indians leaped and sang, their familiar mode of celebrating welcome. They offered to the explorers great quantities of fish and of the bread which they baked from the ripened corn. They brought little children in their arms, making signs for Cartier and his companions to touch them.

As the twilight gathered, the French withdrew to their boats, while the savages, who were loath to leave the spot, lighted huge bonfires on the shore. A striking and weird picture it conjures up before our eyes,—the French sailors with their bronzed and bearded faces, their strange dress and accoutrements, the glare of the great bonfires on the edge of the dark waters, the wild dances of the exultant savages. The romance and inspiration of the history of Canada are suggested by this riotous welcome of the Old World by the New. It meant that mighty changes were pending; the eye of imagination may see in the background the shadowed outline of the spires and steeples of the great city of to-day.

On the next day, October 3, the French were astir with the first light of the morning. A few of their number were left to guard the boats; the others, accompanied by some of the Indians, set out on foot for Hochelaga. Their way lay over a beaten path through the woods. It brought them presently to the tall palisades that surrounded the group of long wooden houses forming the Indian settle-

CARTIER AT HOCHELAGA

ment. It stood just below the slope of the mountain, and covered a space of almost two acres. On the map of the modern city this village of Hochelaga would be bounded by the four streets, Metcalfe, Mansfield, Burnside, and Sherbrooke, just below the site of McGill University. But the visit of Cartier is an event of such historic interest that it can best be narrated in the words of his own narrative. We may follow here as elsewhere the translation of Hakluyt, which is itself three hundred years old, and seems in its quaint and picturesque form more fitting than the commoner garb of modern prose.

Our captain [so runs the narrative], the next day very early in the morning, having very gorgeously attired himself, caused all his company to be set in order to go to see the town and habitation of these people, and a certain mountain that is somewhere near the city; with whom went also five gentlemen and twenty mariners, leaving the rest to keep and look to our boats. We took with us three men of Hochelaga to bring us to the place. All along as we went we found the way as well beaten and frequented as can be, the fairest and best country that can possibly be seen, full of as goodly great oaks as are in any wood in France, under which the ground was all covered over with fair acorns.

After we had gone about four or five miles, we met by the way one of the chiefest lords of the city, accompanied with many more, who, as soon as he saw us, beckoned and made signs upon us, that we must rest in that place where they had made a great fire and so we did. After that we rested ourselves there awhile, the said lord began to make a long discourse, even as we have said above they are accustomed to do in sign of mirth and friendship, showing our captain and all his company a joyful countenance and good will, who gave him two hatchets, a pair of knives and a cross which he made him to kiss, and then put it about his neck, for which he gave our captain hearty thanks. This done, we went along, and about a mile and a half farther, we began to find goodly and large fields full of such corn as the country yieldeth. It is even as the millet of Brazil as great and somewhat bigger than small peason [peas], wherewith they live as we do with ours.

In the midst of those fields is the city

of Hochelaga, placed near and, as it were, joined to a very great mountain, that is tilled round about, very fertile, on the top of which you may see very far. We named it Mount Royal. The city of Hochelaga is round compassed about with timber, with three courses of rampires [stockades], one within another, framed like a sharp spire, but laid across above. The middlemost of them is made and built as a direct line but perpendicular. The rampires are framed and fashioned with pieces of timber laid along on the ground, very well and cunningly joined together after their fashion. This enclosure is in height about two rods. It hath but one gate of entry thereat, which is shut with piles, stakes, and bars. Over it and also in many places of the wall there be places to run along and ladders to get up, all full of stones, for the defence of it.

There are in the town about fifty houses, about fifty paces long, and twelve or fifteen broad, built all of wood, covered over with the bark of the wood as broad as any board, very finely and cunningly joined together. Within the said houses there are many rooms, lodgings and chambers. In the midst of every one there is a great court in the middle whereof they make their fire.

Such is the picture of Hochelaga as Cartier has drawn it for us. Arrived at the palisade, the savages conducted Cartier and his followers within. In the central space of the stockade was a large square, bordered by the lodges of the Indians. In this the French were halted, and the natives gathered about them, the women, many of whom bore children in their arms, pressing close up to the visitors, stroking their faces and arms, and making entreaties by signs that the French should touch their children.

Then presently [writes Cartier] came the women again, every one bringing a four-square mat in the manner of carpets, and spreading them abroad in that place, they caused us to sit upon them. This done the lord and king of the country was brought upon nine or ten men's shoulders (whom in their tongue they call Agouhanna), sitting upon a great stag's skin, and they laid him down upon the foresaid mats near to the captain, every one beckoning unto us that he was their lord and king. This Agouhanna was a man about fifty years old. He was no whit better apparelled than any of the rest, only excepted that he had a certain thing made of hedgehogs [porcupines], like a red wreath, and that was instead of his crown. He was full of the palsy, and his members shrunk together. After he had with certain signs saluted our captain and all his company, and by manifest tokens bid all welcome, he showed his legs and arms to our captain, and with signs desired him to touch them, and so we did, rubbing them with his own hands; then did Agouhanna take the wreath or crown he had about his head, and gave it unto our captain That done, they brought before him divers diseased men, some blind, some crippled, some lame, and some so old that the hair of their eyelids came down and covered their cheeks, and laid them all along before our captain to the end that they might of him be touched. For it seemed unto them that God was descended and come down from heaven to heal them.

Our captain, seeing the misery and devotion of this poor people, recited the Gospel of St John, that is to say, 'IN THE BEGINNING WAS THE WORD,' touching every one that were [*sic*] diseased, praying to God that it would please Him to open the hearts of the poor people and to make them know His Holy Word, and that they might receive baptism and christendom. That done, he took a service-book in his hand, and with a loud voice read all the passion of Christ, word by word, that all the standers-by might hear him; all which while this poor people kept silence and were marvellously attentive, looking up to heaven and imitating us in gestures. Then he caused the men all orderly to be set on one side, the women on another, and likewise the children on another, and to the chiefest of them he gave hatchets, to the others knives, and to the women beads and such other small trifles. Then where the children were he cast rings, counters and brooches made of tin, whereat they seemed to be very glad.

Before Cartier and his men returned to their boats, some of the Indians took them up to the top of Mount Royal. Here a magnificent prospect offered itself, then, as now, to the eye. The broad level of the island swept towards the west, luxuriant with yellow corn and autumn foliage. In the distance the eye discerned the foaming waters of Lachine, and the silver bosom of the Lake of the Two

Mountains: 'as fair and level a country,' said Cartier, 'as possibly can be seen, being level, smooth, and very plain, fit to be husbanded and tilled.'

The Indians, pointing to the west, explained by signs that beyond the rapids were three other great falls of water, and that when these were passed a man might travel for three months up the waters of the great river. Such at least Cartier understood to be the meaning of the Indians. They showed him a second stream, the Ottawa, as great, they said, as the St Lawrence, whose north-westward course Cartier supposed must run through the kingdom of Saguenay. As the savages pointed to the Ottawa, they took hold of a silver chain on which hung the whistle that Cartier carried, and then touched the dagger of one of the sailors, which had a handle of copper, yellow as gold, as if to show that these metals, or rather silver and gold, came from the country beyond that river. This, at least, was the way that Cartier interpreted the simple and evident signs that the Indians made. The commentators on Cartier's voyages have ever since sought some other explanation, supposing that no such metals existed in the country. The discovery of the gold and silver deposits of the basin of the Ottawa in the district of New Ontario shows that Cartier had truly understood the signs of the Indians. If they had ever seen silver before, it is precisely from this country that it would have come. Cartier was given to understand, also, that in this same region there dwelt another race of savages, very fierce, and continually at war.

The party descended from the mountain and pursued their way towards the boats. Their Indian friends hung upon their footsteps, showing evidences of admiration and affection, and even carried in their arms any of the French who showed indications of weariness. They stood about with every sign of grief and regret as the sails were hoisted and the boats bearing the wonderful beings dropped swiftly down the river. On October 4, the boats safely rejoined the *Emerillon* that lay anchored near the mouth of the Richelieu. On the 11th of the same month, the pinnace was back at her anchorage beside Stadacona, and the whole company was safely reunited. The expedition to Hochelaga had been accomplished in twenty-two days.

CHAPTER VII

THE SECOND VOYAGE—WINTER AT STADACONA

On returning to his anchorage before Quebec, Cartier found that his companions whom he had left there had not been idle. The ships, it will be remembered, lay moored close to the shore at the mouth of the little river Lairet, a branch of the St Charles. On the bank of the river, during their leader's absence, the men had erected a solid fortification or rampart. Heavy sticks of lumber had been set up on end and joined firmly together, while at intervals cannon, taken from the ships, had been placed in such a way as to command the approach in all directions. The sequel showed that it was well, indeed, for the French that they placed so little reliance on the friendship of the savages.

Donnacona was not long in putting in an appearance. Whatever may have been his real feelings, the crafty old chief feigned a great delight at the safe return of Cartier. At his solicitation Cartier paid a ceremonial visit to the settlement of Stadacona, on October 13, ten days after his return. The gentlemen of the expedition, together with fifty sailors, all well armed and appointed, accompanied the leader. The meeting between the Indians and their white visitors was similar to those already described. Indian harangues and wild dancing and shouting were the order of the day, while Cartier, as usual, distributed knives and trinkets. The French were taken into the Indian lodges and shown the stores of food laid up against the coming winter. Other objects, too, of a new and peculiar interest were displayed: there were the 'scalp locks' of five men—'the skin of five men's heads,' says Cartier,—which were spread out on a board like parchments. The Indians explained that these had been taken from the heads of five of their deadly enemies, the Toudamani, a fierce people living to the south, with whom the natives of Stadacona were perpetually at war.

A gruesome story was also told of a great massacre of a war party of Donnacona's people who had been on their way down to the Gaspé country. The party, so the story ran, had encamped upon an island near the

WINTER AT STADACONA

Saguenay. They numbered in all two hundred people, women and children being also among the warriors, and were gathered within the shelter of a rude stockade. In the dead of night their enemies broke upon the sleeping Indians in wild assault; they fired the stockade, and those who did not perish in the flames fell beneath the tomahawk. Five only escaped to bring the story to Stadacona. The truth of the story was proved, long after the writing of Cartier's narrative, by the finding of a great pile of human bones in a cave on an island near Bic, not far from the mouth of the Saguenay. The place is called L'Isle au Massacre to-day.

The French now settled down into their winter quarters. They seem for some time to have mingled freely with the Indians of the Stadacona settlement, especially during the month which yet remained before the rigour of winter locked their ships in snow and ice. Cartier, being of an observing and accurate turn of mind, has left in his narrative some interesting notes upon the life and ideas of the savages. They had, he said, no belief in a true God. Their deity, Cudragny, was supposed to tell them the weather, and, if angry, to throw dust into their eyes. They

thought that, when they died, they would
to the stars, and after that, little by litt.
sink with the stars to earth again, to where
the happy hunting grounds lie on the far
horizon of the world. To correct their ignorance, Cartier told them of the true God and of
the verities of the Christian faith. In the end
the savages begged that he would baptize them,
and on at least one occasion a great flock of
them came to him, hoping to be received into
the faith. But Cartier, as he says, having
nobody with him 'who could teach them our
belief and religion,' and doubting, also, the
sincerity of their sudden conversion, put them
off with the promise that at his next coming he
would bring priests and holy oil and cause them
to be baptized.

The Stadacona Indians seem to have lived
on terms of something like community of
goods. Their stock of food—including great
quantities of pumpkins, peas, and corn—was
more or less in common. But, beyond this
and their lodges, their earthly possessions
were few. They dressed somewhat scantily
in skins, and even in the depth of winter were
so little protected from the cold as to excite
the wonder of their observers. Women whose
husbands died never remarried, but went about

with their faces smeared thick with mingled grease and soot.

One peculiar custom of the natives especially attracted the attention of their visitors, and for the oddity of the thing may best be recorded in Cartier's manner. It is an early account of the use of tobacco. 'There groweth also,' he wrote, 'a certain kind of herb, whereof in summer they make a great provision for all the year, making great account of it, and only men use it, and first they cause it to be dried in the sun, then wear it about their necks, wrapped in a little beast's skin made like a little bag, with a hollow piece of wood or stone like a pipe. Then when they please they make powder of it, and then put it in one of the ends of the said cornet or pipe, and laying a coal of fire upon it, at the other end suck so long that they fill their bodies full of smoke till that it cometh out of their mouth and nostrils, even as out of the funnel of a chimney. They say that it doth keep them warm and in health: they never go without some of it about them. We ourselves have tried the same smoke, and, having put it in our mouths, it seemed almost as hot as pepper.'

In spite of the going and coming of the Indians, Cartier from first to last was doubtful of their intentions. Almost every day in the autumn and early winter some of them appeared with eels and fish, glad to exchange them for little trinkets. But the two interpreters endeavoured to make the Indians believe that the things given them by the French were of no value, and Donnacona did his best to get the Indian children out of the hands of the French. Indeed, the eldest of the children, an Indian girl, escaped from the ships and rejoined her people, and it was only with difficulty that Cartier succeeded in getting her back again. Meanwhile a visiting chief, from the country farther inland, gave the French captain to understand that Donnacona and his braves were waiting only an opportunity to overwhelm the ships' company. Cartier kept on his guard. He strengthened the fort with a great moat that ran all round the stockade. The only entry was now by a lifting bridge; and pointed stakes were driven in beside the upright palisade. Fifty men, divided into watches, were kept on guard all night, and, at every change of the watch, the Indians, across the river in their lodges of the Stadacona settlement, could hear the loud sounds of the trumpets break the clear silence of the winter night.

WINTER AT STADACONA

We have no record of the life of Cartier and his followers during the winter of their isolation among the snows and the savages of Quebec. It must, indeed, have been a season of dread. The northern cold was soon upon them in all its rigour. The ships were frozen in at their moorings from the middle of November till April 15. The ice lay two fathoms thick in the river, and the driving snows and great drifts blotted out under the frozen mantle of winter all sight of land and water. The French could scarcely stir from their quarters. Their fear of Indian treachery and their ignorance of the trackless country about them held them imprisoned in their ships. A worse peril was soon added. The scourge of scurvy was laid upon them—an awful disease, hideous in its form and deadly in its effect. Originating in the Indian camp, it spread to the ships. In December fifty of the Stadacona Indians died, and by the middle of February, of the hundred and ten men that made up Cartier's expedition, only three or four remained in health. Eight were already dead, and their bodies, for want of burial, lay frozen stark beneath the snowdrifts of the river, hidden from the prying eyes of the savages. Fifty more lay at the point of death, and the others, crippled and staggering with the onslaught of disease, moved to and fro at their tasks, their fingers numbed with cold, their hearts frozen with despair.

The plague that had fallen upon them was such as none of them had ever before seen. The legs of the sufferers swelled to huge, unsightly, and livid masses of flesh. Their sinews shrivelled to blackened strings, pimpled with purple clots of blood. The awful disease worked its way upwards. The arms hung hideous and useless at the side, the mouth rotted till the teeth fell from the putrid flesh. Chilled with the cold, huddled in the narrow holds of the little ships fast frozen in the endless desolation of the snow, the agonized sufferers breathed their last, remote from aid, far from the love of women, and deprived of the consolations of the Church. Let those who realize the full horror of the picture think well upon what stout deeds the commonwealth of Canada has been founded.

Without the courage and resource of their leader, whose iron constitution kept him in full health, all would have been lost. Cartier spared no efforts. The knowledge of his situation was concealed from the Indians. None were allowed aboard the ships, and, as

WINTER AT STADACONA

as might be, a great clatter of hammering was kept up whenever the Indians appeared in sight, so that they might suppose that Cartier's men were forced by the urgency of their tasks to remain on the ships. Nor was spiritual aid neglected. An image of the Virgin Mary was placed against a tree about a bow-shot from the fort, and to this all who could walk betook themselves in procession on the Sunday when the sickness was at its height. They moved in solemn order, singing as they went the penitential psalms and the Litany, and imploring the intercession of the Virgin. Thus passed the days until twenty-five of the French had been laid beneath the snow. For the others there seemed only the prospect of death from disease or of destruction at the hands of the savages.

It happened one day that Cartier was walking up and down by himself upon the ice when he saw a band of Indians coming over to him from Stadacona. Among them was the interpreter Domagaya, whom Cartier had known to be stricken by the illness only ten days before, but who now appeared in abundant health. On being asked the manner of his cure, the interpreter told Cartier that he had been healed by a beverage made from the leaves and bark of a tree. Cartier, as we have seen, had kept from the Indians the knowledge of his troubles, for he dared not disclose the real weakness of the French. Now, feigning that only a servant was ill, he asked for details of the remedy, and, when he did so, the Indians sent their women to fetch branches of the tree in question. The bark and leaves were to be boiled, and the drink thus made was to be taken twice a day. The potion was duly administered, and the cure that it effected was so rapid and so complete that the pious Cartier declared it a real and evident miracle. 'If all the doctors of Lorraine and Montpellier had been there with all the drugs of Alexandria,' he wrote, 'they could not have done as much in a year as the said tree did in six days.' An entire tree—probably a white spruce—was used up in less than eight days. The scourge passed and the sailors, now restored to health, eagerly awaited the coming of the spring.

Meanwhile the cold lessened; the ice about the ships relaxed its hold, and by the middle of April they once more floated free. But a new anxiety had been added. About the time when the fortunes of Cartier's company were at their lowest, Donnacona had left his camp with certain of his followers, ostensibly

WINTER AT STADACONA

to spend a fortnight in hunting deer in the forest. For two months he did not return. When he came back, he was accompanied not only by Taignoagny and his own braves, but by a great number of savages, fierce and strong, whom the French had never before seen. Cartier was assured that treachery was brewing, and he determined to forestall it. He took care that his men should keep away from the settlement of Stadacona, but he sent over his servant, Charles Guyot, who had endeared himself to the Indians during the winter. Guyot reported that the lodges were filled with strange faces, that Donnacona had pretended to be sick and would not show himself, and that he himself had been received with suspicion, Taignoagny having forbidden him to enter into some of the houses.

Cartier's plan was soon made. The river was now open and all was ready for departure. Rather than allow himself and his men to be overwhelmed by an attack of the great concourse of warriors who surrounded the settlement of Stadacona, he determined to take his leave in his own way and at his own time, and to carry off with him the leaders of the savages themselves. Following the custom of his age, he did not wish to return without the visible signs of his achievements. Donnacona ha freely boasted to him of the wonders of the great country far up beyond Hochelaga, of lands where gold and silver existed in abundance, where the people dressed like the French in woollen clothes, and of even greater wonders still,—of men with no stomachs, and of a race of beings with only one leg. These things were of such import, Cartier thought, that they merited narration to the king of France himself. If Donnacona had actually seen them, it was fitting that he should describe them in the august presence of Francis I.

The result was a plot which succeeded. The two ships, the *Grande Hermine* and the *Emerillon*, lay at anchor ready to sail. Owing to the diminished numbers of his company, Cartier had decided to abandon the third ship. He announced a final ceremony to signalize the approaching departure. On May 3, 1536, a tall cross, thirty-five feet high was planted on the river bank. Beneath the cross-bar it carried the arms of France, and on the upper part a scroll in ancient lettering that read, 'FRANCISCUS PRIMUS DEI GRATIA FRANCORUM REX REGNAT,' which means, freely translated, 'Francis I, by the grace of God King of the French, is sovereign.'

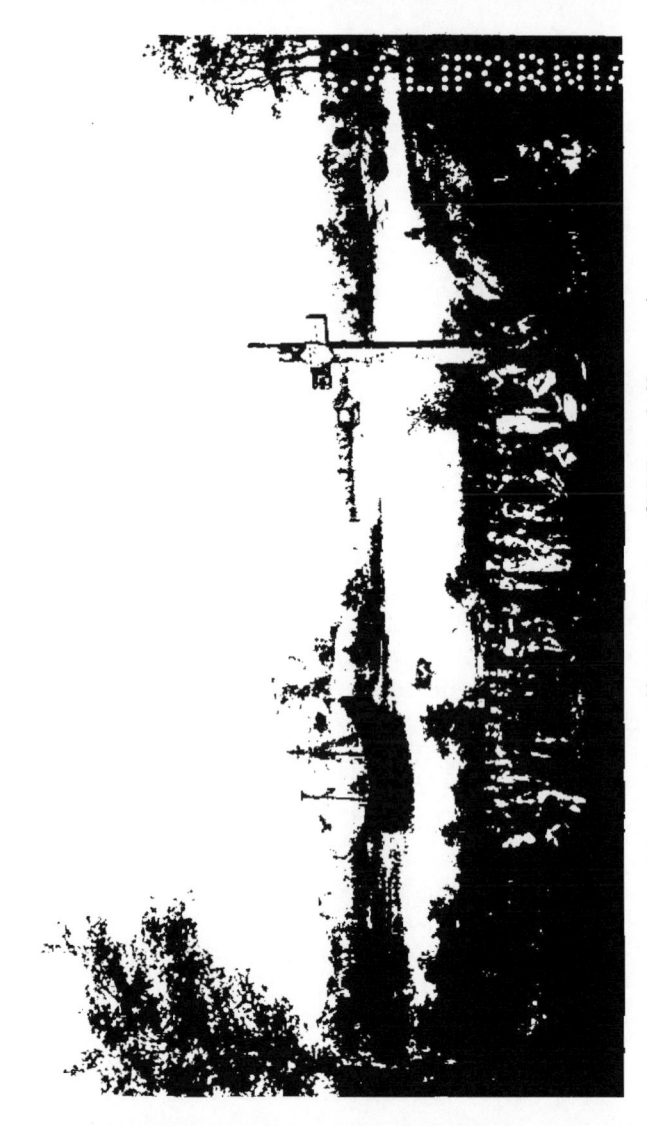

THE FINAL CEREMONY AT QUEBEC, MAY 3, 1536

From an old engraving

WINTER AT STADACONA

Donnacona, Taignoagny, Domagaya and a few others, who had been invited to come on board the ships, found themselves the prisoners of the French. At first rage and consternation seized upon the savages, deprived by this stratagem of their chief. They gathered in great numbers on the bank, and their terrifying howls and war-cries resounded throughout the night. But Donnacona, whether from simplicity or craft, let himself be pacified with new presents and with the promise of a speedy return in the year following. He showed himself on the deck of the captain's ship, and his delighted followers gathered about in their canoes and swore renewed friendship with the white men, whom they had, in all likelihood, plotted to betray. Gifts were exchanged, and the French bestowed a last shower of presents on the assembled Indians. Finally, on May 6, the caravels dropped down the river, and the homeward voyage began.

The voyage passed without incident. The ships were some time in descending the St Lawrence. At Isle-aux-Coudres they waited for the swollen tide of the river to abate. The Indians still flocked about them in canoes, talking with Donnacona and his men, but powerless to effect a rescue of the chief. Contrary winds held the vessels until, at last, on May 21, fair winds set in from the west that carried them in an easy run to the familiar coast of Gaspé, past Brion Island, through the passage between Newfoundland and the Cape Breton shore, and so outward into the open Atlantic.

'On July 6, 1536,' so ends Cartier's chronicle of this voyage, 'we reached the harbour of St Malo, by the Grace of our Creator, whom we pray, making an end of our navigation, to grant us His Grace, and Paradise at the end. Amen.'

CHAPTER VIII

THE THIRD VOYAGE

NEARLY five years elapsed after Cartier's return to St Malo before he again set sail for the New World. His royal master, indeed, had received him most graciously. Francis had deigned to listen with pleasure to the recital of his pilot's adventures, and had ordered him to set them down in writing. Moreover, he had seen and conversed with Donnacona and the other captive Indians, who had told of the wonders of their distant country. The Indians had learned the language of their captors and spoke with the king in French. Francis gave orders that they should be received into the faith, and the registers of St Malo show that on March 25, 1538, or 1539 (the year is a little uncertain), there were baptized three savages from Canada brought from the said country by ' honnete homme [honest man], Jacques Cartier, captain of our Lord the King.'

But the moment was unsuited for further

endeavour in the New World. Francis had enough to do to save his own soil from the invading Spaniard. Nor was it until the king of France on June 15, 1538, made a truce with his inveterate foe, Charles V, that he was able to turn again to American discovery. Profoundly impressed with the vast extent and unbounded resources of the countries described in Cartier's narrative, the king decided to assume the sovereignty of this new land, and to send out for further discovery an expedition of some magnitude. At the head of it he placed Jean François de la Roque, Sieur de Roberval, whom, on January 15, 1540, he created Lord of Norumbega, viceroy and lieutenant-general of Canada, Hochelaga, Saguenay, Newfoundland, Belle Isle, Carpunt, Labrador, the Great Bay, and Baccalaos. The name Norumbega is an Indian word, and was used by early explorers as a general term for the territory that is now Maine, New Brunswick, and Nova Scotia. Baccalaos is the name often given by the French to Newfoundland, the word itself being of Basque origin and meaning ' codfish,' while Carpunt will be remembered as a harbour beside Belle Isle, where Cartier had been stormbound on his first voyage.

THE THIRD VOYAGE

The king made every effort to further Roberval's expedition. The Lord of Norumbega was given 45,000 lívres and full authority to enlist sailors and colonists for his expedition. The latter appears to have been a difficult task, and, after the custom of the day, recourse was presently had to the prisons to recruit the ranks of the prospective settlers. Letters were issued to Roberval authorizing him to search the jails of Paris, Toulouse, Bordeaux, Rouen, and Dijon and to draw from them any convicts lying under sentence of death. Exception was made of heretics, traitors, and counterfeiters, as unfitted for the pious purpose of the voyage. The gangs of these miscreants, chained together and under guard, came presently trooping into St Malo. Among them, it is recorded, walked a young girl of eighteen, unconvicted of any crime, who of her own will had herself chained to a malefactor, as hideous physically as morally, whose lot she was determined to share.

To Roberval, as commander of the enterprise, was attached Cartier in the capacity of captain-general and master-pilot. The letters patent which contain the appointment speak of him as our 'dear and well-beloved Jacques Cartier, who has discovered the large countries of Canada and Hochelaga which lie at the end of Asia.' Cartier received from Roberval about 31,300 livres. The king gave to him for this voyage the little ship *Emerillon* and commanded him to obtain four others and to arm and equip the five. The preparations for the voyage seem to have lasted throughout the winter and spring of the years 1540-41. The king had urged Cartier to start by the middle of April, but it was not until May 23, 1541, that the ships were actually able to set sail. Even then Roberval was not ready to leave. Cannon, powder, and a varied equipment that had been purchased for the voyage were still lying at various points in Normandy and Champagne. Cartier, anxious to follow the king's wishes, could wait no longer and, at length, he set out with his five ships, leaving Roberval to prepare other ships at Honfleur and follow as he might. From first to last the relations of Cartier and Roberval appear to need further explanation than that which we possess. Roberval was evidently the nominal head of the enterprise and the feudal lord of the countries to be claimed, but Cartier seems to have been restless under any attempt to dictate the actual plan to be adopted, and his final desertion of Roberval may be ascribed to the

THE THIRD VOYAGE

position in which he was placed by the divided command of the expedition.

The expedition left St Malo on May 23, 1541, bearing in the ships food and victuals for two years. The voyage was unprosperous. Contrary winds and great gales raged over the Atlantic. The ships were separated at sea, and before they reached the shores of Newfoundland were so hard put to it for fresh water that it was necessary to broach the cider casks to give drink to the goats and the cattle which they carried. But the ships came together presently in safety in the harbour of Carpunt beside Belle Isle, refitted there, and waited vainly for Roberval. They finally reached the harbour of the Holy Cross at Stadacona on August 23.

The savages flocked to meet the ships with a great display of joy, looking eagerly for the return of their vanished Donnacona. Their new chief, Agouhanna, with six canoes filled with men, women, and children, put off from the shore. The moment was a difficult one. Donnacona and all his fellow-captives, except only one little girl, had died in France. Cartier dared not tell the whole truth to the natives, and he contented himself with saying that Donnacona was dead, but that the other

Indians had become great lords in France, had married there and did not wish to return. Whatever may have been the feeling of the tribe at this tale, the new chief at least was well pleased. 'I think,' wrote Cartier, in his narrative of this voyage, 'he took it so well because he remained lord and governor of the country by the death of the said Donnacona.' Agouhanna certainly made a great show of friendliness. He took from his own head the ornament of hide and wampum that he wore and bound it round the brows of the French leader. At the same time he put his arms about his neck with every sign of affection.

When the customary ceremonies of eating and drinking, speech-making, and presentations had ended, Cartier, after first exploring with his boats, sailed with his ships a few miles above Stadacona to a little river where good anchorage was found, now known as the Cap Rouge river. It enters the St Lawrence a little above Quebec. Here preparations were at once made for the winter's sojourn. Cannon were brought ashore from three of the ships. A strong fort was constructed, and the little settlement received the pretentious name Charlesbourg Royal. The remaining part of the month of August 1541 was spent in

THE THIRD VOYAGE

making fortifications and in unloading the ships. On September 2 two of the ships, commanded by Mace Jalobert, Cartier's brother-in-law and companion of the preceding voyage, and Etienne Nouel, his nephew, were sent back to France to tell the king of what had been done, and to let him know that Roberval had not yet arrived.

As on his preceding voyages, Cartier was greatly impressed by the aspect of the country about him. All round were splendid forests of oak and maple and cedar and beech, which surpassed even the beautiful woodlands of France. Grape vines loaded with ripe fruit hung like garlands from the trees. Nor was the forest thick and tangled, but rather like an open park, so that among the trees were great stretches of ground wanting only to be tilled. Twenty of Cartier's men were set to turn the soil, and in one day had prepared and sown about an acre and a half of ground. The cabbage, lettuce, and turnip seed that they planted showed green shoots within a week.

At the mouth of the Cap Rouge river there is a high point, now called Redclyffe. On this Cartier constructed a second fort, which commanded the fortification and the ships below. A little spring supplied fresh water, and the natural situation afforded a protection against attack by water or by land. While the French laboured in building the stockades and in hauling provisions and equipments from the ships to the forts, they made other discoveries that impressed them more than the forest wealth of this new land. Close beside the upper fort they found in the soil a good store of stones which they 'esteemed to be diamonds.' At the foot of the slope along the St Lawrence lay iron deposits, and the sand of the shore needed only, Cartier said, to be put into the furnace to get the iron from it. At the water's edge they found 'certain leaves of fine gold as thick as a man's nail,' and in the slabs of black slate-stone which ribbed the open glades of the wood there were veins of mineral matter which shone like gold and silver. Cartier's mineral discoveries have unfortunately not resulted in anything. We know now that his diamonds, still to be seen about Cap Rouge, are rock crystals. The gold which he later on showed to Roberval, and which was tested, proved genuine enough, but the quantity of such deposits in the region has proved insignificant. It is very likely that Cartier would make the most of his mineral

THE THIRD VOYAGE

discoveries as the readiest means of exciting his master's interest.

When everything was in order at the settlement, the provisions landed, and the building well under way, the leader decided to make a brief journey to Hochelaga, in order to view more narrowly the rapids that he had seen, and to be the better able to plan an expedition into the interior for the coming spring. The account of this journey is the last of Cartier's exploits of which we have any detailed account, and even here the closing pages of his narrative are unsatisfactory and inconclusive. What is most strange is that, although he expressly says that he intended to 'go as far as Hochelaga, of purpose to view and understand the fashion of the saults [falls] of water,' he makes no mention of the settlement of Hochelaga itself, and does not seem to have visited it.

The Hochelaga expedition, in which two boats were used, left the camp at Cap Rouge on September 7, 1541. A number of Cartier's gentlemen accompanied him on the journey, while the Viscount Beaupré was left behind in command of the fort. On their way up the river Cartier visited the chief who had entrusted his little daughter to the care of the French at Stadacona at the time of Cartier's wintering there. He left two young French boys in charge of this Indian chief that they might learn the language of the country. No further episode of the journey is chronicled until on September 11 the boats arrived at the foot of the rapids now called Lachine. Cartier tells us that two leagues from the foot of the bottom fall was an Indian village called Tutonaguy, but he does not say whether or not this was the same place as the Hochelaga of his previous voyage. The French left their boats and, conducted by the Indians, walked along the portage path that led past the rapids. There were large encampments of natives beside the second fall, and they received the French with every expression of good-will. By placing little sticks upon the ground they gave Cartier to understand that a third rapid was to be passed, and that the river was not navigable to the country of Saguenay.

Convinced that further exploration was not possible for the time being, the French returned to their boats. As usual, a great concourse of Indians had come to the spot. Cartier says that he 'understood afterwards' that the Indians would have made an end of the French, but judged them too strong for

THE THIRD VOYAGE

the attempt. The expedition started at once for the winter quarters at Cap Rouge. As they passed Hochelay—the abode of the supposed friendly chief near Portneuf—they learned that he had gone down the river ahead of them to devise means with Agouhanna for the destruction of the expedition.

Cartier's narrative ends at this most dramatic moment of his adventures. He seems to have reached the encampment at Cap Rouge at the very moment when an Indian assault was imminent. We know, indeed, that the attack, which, from certain allusions in the narrative, seems presently to have been made, was warded off, and that Cartier's ships and a part at least of his company sailed home to France, falling in with Roberval on the way. But the story of the long months of anxiety and privation, and probably of disease and hostilities with the Indians, is not recorded. The narrative of the great explorer, as it is translated by Hakluyt, closes with the following ominous sentences:

'And when we were arrived at our fort, we understood by our people that the savages of the country came not any more about our fort, as they were accustomed, to bring us fish, and that they were in a wonderful doubt and fear of us. Wherefore our captain, having been advised by some of our men which had been at Stadacona to visit them that there was a wonderful number of the country people assembled together, caused all things in our fortress to be set in good order.' And beyond these words, Cartier's story was never written, or, if written, it has been lost.

CHAPTER IX

THE CLOSE OF CARTIER'S CAREER

GREAT doubt and uncertainty surround the ultimate fate of Roberval's attempted colony, of which Cartier's expedition was to form the advance guard. Roberval, as already seen, had stayed behind in France when Cartier sailed in 1541, because his equipment was not yet ready for the voyage. Nor does he seem to have finally started on his expedition for nearly a year after the departure of Cartier. It has been suggested that Roberval did set sail at some time in the summer of 1541, and that he reached Cape Breton island and built a fort there. So, at least, a tradition ran that was repeated many years later by Lescarbot in his *Histoire de la Nouvelle France*. If this statement is true, it must mean that Roberval sailed home again at the close of 1541, without having succeeded in finding Cartier, and that he prepared for a renewed expedition in the spring of the coming year.

But the evidence for any such voyage is not conclusive.

What we know is that on April 16, 1542, Roberval sailed out of the port of Rochelle with three tall ships and a company of two hundred persons, men and women, and that with him were divers gentlemen of quality. On June 8, 1542, his ships entered the harbour of St John's in Newfoundland. They found there seventeen fishing vessels, clear proof that by this time the cod fisheries of the Newfoundland Banks were well known. They were, indeed, visited by the French, the Portuguese, and other nations. Here Roberval paused to refit his ships and to replenish his stores. While he was still in the harbour, one day, to his amazement, Cartier sailed in with the five ships that he was bringing away from his abandoned settlement at Charlesbourg Royal. Cartier showed to his superior the 'diamonds' and the gold that he was bringing home from Canada. He gave to Roberval a glowing account of the country that he had seen, but, according to the meagre details that appear in the fragment in Hakluyt's *Voyages*, he made clear that he had been compelled to abandon his attempt at settlement. 'He could not with his small company

THE CLOSE OF CARTIER'S CAREER

withstand the savages, which went about daily to annoy him, which was the cause of his return into France.'

Except what is contained in the few sentences of this record we know nothing of what took place between Roberval and Cartier. But it was quite clear that the latter considered the whole enterprise as doomed to failure. It is more than likely that Cartier was dissatisfied with Roberval's delay, and did not care to continue under the orders of a leader inferior to himself in capacity. Be this as it may, their final parting stands recorded in the following terms, and no historical document has as yet come to light which can make the exact situation known to us. 'When our general [Roberval], being furnished with sufficient forces, commanded him [Cartier] to go back with him, he and his company, moved as it seems with ambition, because they would have all the glory of the discovery of those parts themselves, stole privily away the next night from us, and, without taking their leaves, departed home for Brittany.' The story, it must be remembered, comes from the pen of either Roberval or one of his associates.

The subsequent history of Roberval's colony, as far as it is known, can be briefly told. His ships reached the site of Charlesbourg Royal late in July 1542. He landed stores and munitions and erected houses, apparently on a scale of some magnitude, with towers and fortifications and with great kitchens, halls, and living rooms. Two ships were sent home in the autumn with news of the expedition, their leader being especially charged to find out whether the rock crystals carried back by Cartier had turned out to be diamonds. All the other colonists remained and spent the winter in this place. In spite of their long preparation and of their commodious buildings, they seem to have endured sufferings as great as, or even greater than, those of Cartier's men at Stadacona seven years before. Supplies of food ran short, and even in the autumn before the stern winter had begun it was necessary to put the whole company on carefully measured rations. Disease broke out among the French, as it had broken out under Cartier, and about fifty of their number perished before the coming of the spring. Their lot was rendered more dreadful still by quarrelling and crime. Roberval could keep his colonists in subjection only by the use of irons and by the application of the lash. The gibbet, reared beside the fort, claimed its toll of their number.

THE CLOSE OF CARTIER'S CAREER

The winter of their misery drew slowly to its close. The ice of the river began to break in April. On June 5, 1543, their leader, Roberval, embarked on an expedition to explore the Saguenay, 'leaving thirty persons behind in the fort, with orders that if Roberval had not returned by the first of July, they were to depart for France.' Whither he went and what he found we do not know. We read that on June 14 certain of his company came back with messages to the fort: that five days later still others came back with instructions that the company at the fort were to delay their departure for France until July 19. And here the narrative of the colony breaks off.

Of Roberval's subsequent fate we can learn hardly anything. There is some evidence to show that Cartier was dispatched from France to Canada to bring him back. Certain it is that in April 1544 orders were issued for the summons of both Cartier and Roberval to appear before a commission for the settling of their accounts. The report of the royal auditors credits Cartier apparently with a service of eight months spent in returning to Canada to bring Roberval home. On the strength of this, it is thought likely that Cartier, returning safely to France in the summer of 1542, was sent back again at the king's command to aid in the return of the colonists, whose enterprise was recognized as a failure. After this, Roberval is lost to sight in the history of France. Certain chroniclers have said that he made another voyage to the New World and perished at sea. Others have it that he was assassinated in Paris near the church of the Holy Innocents. But nothing is known.

Cartier also is practically lost from sight during the last fifteen years of his life. His name appears at intervals in the local records, notably on the register of baptisms as a godfather. As far as can be judged, he spent the remainder of his days in comfortable retirement in his native town of St Malo. Besides his house in the seaport he had a country residence some miles distant at Limoilou. This old house of solid and substantial stone, with a courtyard and stone walls surrounding it, is still standing. There can be no doubt that the famous pilot enjoyed during his closing years a universal esteem. It is just possible that in recognition of his services he was elevated in rank by the king of France, for in certain records of St Malo in 1549, he is spoken of as the Sieur de Limoilou. But this

CARTIER'S MANOR HOUSE AT LIMOILOU, NEAR ST MALO

From 'Brief Récit' of Jacques Cartier

THE CLOSE OF CARTIER'S CAREER

may have been merely the sort of courtesy title often given in those days to the proprietors of small landed estates.

It was sometimes the custom of the officials of the port of St Malo to mark down in the records of the day the death of any townsman of especial note. Such an entry as this is the last record of the great pilot. In the margins of certain documents of September 1, 1557, there is written in the quaint, almost unreadable penmanship of the time: 'This said Wednesday about five in the morning died Jacques Cartier.'

There is no need to enlarge upon the greatness of Cartier's achievements. It was only the beginning of a far-reaching work, the completion of which fell to other hands. But it is Cartier's proud place in history to bear the title of discoverer of a country whose annals were later to be illumined by the exploits of a Champlain and a La Salle, and the martyrdom of a Brébeuf; which was to witness, for more than half a century, a conflict in arms between Great Britain and France, and from that conflict to draw the finest pages of its history and the noblest inspiration of its future; a country upon whose soil, majestic in its expanse of river, lake, and forest, was to be reared a commonwealth built upon the union and harmony of the two great races who had fought for its dominion.

Jacques Cartier, as much perhaps as any man of his time, embodied in himself what was highest in the spirit of his age. He shows us the daring of the adventurer with nothing of the dark cruelty by which such daring was often disfigured. He brought to his task the simple faith of the Christian whose devout fear of God renders him fearless of the perils of sea and storm. The darkest hour of his adversity in that grim winter at Stadacona found him still undismayed. He came to these coasts to find a pathway to the empire of the East. He found instead a country vast and beautiful beyond his dreams. The enthusiasm of it entered into his soul. Asia was forgotten before the reality of Canada. Since Cartier's day four centuries of history have hallowed the soil of Canada with memories and associations never to be forgotten. But patriotism can find no finer example than the instinctive admiration and love called forth in the heart of Jacques Cartier by the majestic beauty of the land of which he was the discoverer.

ITINERARY OF CARTIER'S VOYAGES

Adapted from Baxter's 'Memoir of Jacques Cartier'

VOYAGE OF 1534

April 20	Monday	Cartier leaves St Malo.
May 10	Sunday	Arrives at Bonavista.
,, 21	Thursday	Reaches Isle of Birds.
,, 24	Sunday	Enters the harbour of Kirpon.
June 9	Tuesday	Leaves Kirpon.
,, 10	Wednesday	Enters the harbour of Brest.
,, 11	Thursday	St Barnabas Day. Hears Mass and explores coast in boats.
,, 12	Friday	Names St Anthoine, Servan; plants cross and names river St Jacques, and harbour Jacques Cartier.
,, 13	Saturday	Returns to ships.
,, 14	Sunday	Hears Mass.
,, 15	Monday	Sails toward north coast of Newfoundland.
,, 16	Tuesday	Follows the west coast of Newfoundland and names the Monts des Granches.

June 17	Wednesday	Names the Colombiers, Bay St Julien, and Capes Royal and Milk.
,, 18	Thursday	Stormy weather to 24th; explores coast between Capes Royal and Milk.
,, 24	Wednesday	Festival of St John the Baptist. Names Cape St John.
,, 25	Thursday and	Weather bad; sails toward the west and southwest; discovers Isles Margaux, Brion, and Cape Dauphin.
,, 26	Friday	
,, 27	Saturday	Coasts toward west-south-west.
,, 28	Sunday	Reaches Cape Rouge.
,, 29	Monday	Festival of St Peter. Names Alezay and Cape St Peter, and continues course west-south-west.
,, 30	Tuesday	Towards evening descries land appearing like two islands.
July 1	Wednesday	Names Capes Orleans and Savages.
,, 2	Thursday	Names Bay St Leonarius.
,, 3	Friday	Continues northerly course and names Cape Hope.
,, 4	Saturday	Arrives at Port Daniel; remains there until 12th.

ITINERARY OF CARTIER'S VOYAGES 115

July 16 Thursday   Enters Gaspé Bay, and remains until 25th on account of storm.
,, 22 Wednesday Lands and meets savages.
,, 24 Friday   Plants a cross.
,, 25 Saturday   Sets sail with good wind toward Anticosti.
,, 27 Monday   Approaches coast.
,, 28 Tuesday   Names Cape St Louis.
,, 29 Wednesday Names Cape Montmorency and doubles East Cape of Anticosti.
Aug. 1 Saturday   Sights northern shore of the Gulf of St Lawrence.
,, 8 Saturday   Approaches west coast of Newfoundland.
,, 9 Sunday   Arrives at Blanc Sablon, and makes preparations to return home.
,, 15 Saturday   Festival of the Assumption. Hears Mass and sets sail for France.
Sept. 5 Saturday   Arrives at St Malo.

Second Voyage, 1535

May 16 Sunday   First Pentecost. The crew commune at Cathedral and receive Episcopal Benediction.
,, 19 Wednesday Departure from St Malo.
,, 26 Wednesday Contrary winds.

June	25 Friday	Ships separated by storm.
July	7 Wednesday	Cartier reaches the Isle of Birds.
,,	8 Thursday	Enters Strait of Belle Isle.
,,	15 Thursday	Reaches the rendezvous at Blanc Sablon.
,,	26 Monday	Ships meet.
,,	29 Thursday	Follows north coast and names Isles St William.
,,	30 Friday	Names Isles St Marthy.
,,	31 Saturday	Names Cape St Germain.
Aug.	1 Sunday	Contrary winds; enters St Nicholas Harbour.
,,	8 Sunday	Sails toward the southern coast.
,,	9 Monday	Contrary wind; turns toward north and stops in Bay St Lawrence.
,,	13 Friday	Leaves Bay St Lawrence, approaches Anticosti, and doubles the western point.
,,	15 Sunday	Festival of the Assumption. Names Anticosti, Isle of the Assumption.
,,	16 Monday	Continues along coast.
,,	17 Tuesday	Turns toward the north.
,,	19 Thursday	Arrives at the Seven Islands.
,,	20 Friday	Ranges coast with his boats.
,,	21 Saturday	Sails west, but obliged to return to the Seven Islands owing to head winds.

ITINERARY OF CARTIER'S VOYAGES

Aug. 24	Tuesday	Leaves the Seven Islands and sets sail toward south.
,, 29	Sunday	Martyrdom of St John Baptist. Reaches harbour of Isles St John.
Sept. 1	Wednesday	Quits the harbour and directs his course toward the Saguenay.
,, 2	Thursday	Leaves the Saguenay and reaches the Bic Islands.
,, 6	Monday	Arrives at Isle-aux-Coudres.
,, 7	Tuesday	Reaches Island of Orleans.
,, 9	Thursday	Donnacona visits Cartier.
,, 13	Monday	Sails toward the River St Charles.
,, 14	Tuesday	Exaltation of the Holy Cross. Reaches entrance of St Charles River.
,, 15	Wednesday	Plants buoys to guide his ships.
,, 16	Thursday	Two ships are laid up for the winter.
,, 17	Friday	Donnacona tries to dissuade Cartier from going to Hochelaga.
,, 18	Saturday	Donnacona's stratagem to deter Cartier from going to Stadacona.
,, 19	Sunday	Cartier starts for Hochelaga with his pinnace and two boats.

THE MARINER OF ST MALO

Sept. 28	Tuesday	Enters Lake St Peter.
,, 29	Wednesday	Leaves his pinnace, and proceeds with his boats.
Oct. 2	Saturday	Arrives at Hochelaga.
,, 3	Sunday	Lands and visits town and mountain, which he named Mount Royal, and leaves Sunday.
,, 4	Monday	Regains his pinnace.
,, 5	Tuesday	Takes his way back to Stadacona.
,, 7	Thursday	Stops at Three Rivers, and plants cross upon an island.
,, 11	Monday	Arrives at the anchorage beside Stadacona.
,, 12	Tuesday	Donnacona visits Cartier.
,, 13	Wednesday	Cartier and some of his men visit Stadacona.

1536

April 16	Sunday	Easter Sunday. The river clear of ice.
,, 22	Saturday	Donnacona visits Cartier with large number of savages.
,, 28	Friday	Cartier sends Guyot to Stadacona.
May 3	Wednesday	Festival of the Holy Cross. A cross planted; Cartier seizes Donnacona.

ITINERARY OF CARTIER'S VOYAGES

May 5 Friday		The people of Stadacona bring provisions for Cartier's captives.
,, 6 Saturday		Cartier sails.
,, 7 Sunday		Arrives at Isle-aux-Coudres.
,, 15 Monday		Exchanges presents with the savages.
,, 22 Monday		Reaches Isle Brion.
,, 25 Thursday		Festival of the Ascension. Reaches a low, sandy island.
,, 26 Friday		Returns to Isle Brion.
June 1 Thursday		Names Capes Lorraine and St Paul.
,, 4 Sunday		Fourth of Pentecost. Names harbour of St Esprit.
,, 6 Tuesday		Departs from the harbour of St Esprit.
,, 11 Sunday		St Barnabas Day. At Isles St Pierre.
,, 16 Friday		Departs from Isles St Pierre and makes harbour at Rougenouse.
,, 19 Monday		Leaves Rougenouse and sails for home.
July 6 Friday		Reaches St Malo.

Third Voyage, 1541

May 23 Monday		Cartier leaves St Malo with five ships.

Aug. 23	Tuesday	Arrives before Stadacona.
,, 25	Thursday	Lands artillery.
Sept. 2	Friday	Sends two of his ships home.
,, 7	Wednesday	Sets out for Hochelaga.
,, 11	Sunday	Arrives at Lachine Rapids.

(The rest of the voyage is unknown.)

BIBLIOGRAPHICAL NOTE

A GREAT many accounts of the voyages of Jacques Cartier have been written both in French and in English; but the fountain source of information for all of these is found in the narratives written by Cartier himself. The story of the first voyage was written under the name of *Relation Originale du Voyage de Jacques Cartier au Canada en 1534*. The original manuscript was lost from sight for over three hundred years, but about half a century ago it was discovered in the Imperial Library (now the National Library) at Paris. Its contents, however, had long been familiar to English readers through the translation which appears in Hakluyt's *Voyages*, published in 1600. In the same collection is also found the narrative of the second voyage, as translated from the *Bref Recit* written by Cartier and published in 1545, and the fragment of the account of the third voyage of which the rest is lost. For an exhaustive bibliography of Cartier's voyages see Baxter, *A Memoir of Jacques Cartier* (New York, 1906). An exceedingly interesting little book is Sir Joseph Pope's *Jacques Cartier: His Life and*

Voyages (Ottawa, 1890). The student is also recommended to read *The Saint Lawrence Basin and its Borderlands*, by Samuel Edward Dawson; papers by the Abbé Verreau, John Reade, Bishop Howley and W. F. Ganong in the *Transactions of the Royal Society of Canada*; the chapter, 'Jacques Cartier and his Successors,' by B. F. de Costa, in Winsor's *Narrative and Critical History of America*, and the chapter 'The Beginnings of Canada,' by Arthur G. Doughty, in the first volume of *Canada and its Provinces* (Toronto, 1913).

INDEX

Agouhanna, Indian chief at Stadacona, 97, 98.
Anguille, Cape, called by Cartier Cape St John, 23.
Anticosti, 36, 37, 38, 45, 47.

Baccalaos, name given by the French to Newfoundland, 94.
Beaupré, Viscount, commander of fort at Cap Rouge, 101.
Belle Isle, Strait of, 16, 17, 45.
Bic Islands, 50.
Blanc Sablon, 17, 39.
Bonavista, Cape, 12, 13.
Brest, harbour, 17; fort and settlement at, 17.

Cap-des-Rosiers, medallion of Cartier found at, 3-4.
Cap-des-Sauvages, 28.
Cap Rouge river, Cartier's third expedition winters at, 98, 99; Cartier attacked by Indians at, 103.
Cartier, Jacques, portraits of, 1-4; birth, family history, marriage, 6, 7; little knowledge of before becoming a master-pilot, 8-11; sets out on first voyage of exploration, 12; first opinions of New Land, 19, 20; discovers Brion Island, 25-7; first trading with natives, 31; plants a cross with the fleurs-de-lis of France at Gaspé, 34-6; takes two young Indians to France, 36; ships and company of second voyage, 42; reaches Newfoundland, 44; navigates and charts Strait of Belle Isle 45; ascends the St Lawrence, 49, 50, 67; reaches Hochelaga, 69; describes Hochelaga and its people, 71-6; returns to Stadacona, 78; efforts to convert Indians, 82; describes Indians' use of tobacco, 83; strengthens his stockade, 84; carries off Donnacona and two interpreters to France, 91; made captain-general and master-pilot under Roberval, 95; sails without Roberval, 96; again visits Hochelaga, 101; meets Roberval at St John's, 106; returns to France, 107; sent out again to find Roberval, 109; dies at St Malo, 111; his courage and devotion, 112.
Castle Bay, 17.
Chaleur Bay, named by Cartier, 33.

Charlevoix, theory as to name Saguenay, 46.
Cudragny, an Indian deity, 64.
Cumberland Harbour, first named Jacques Cartier Harbour, 19.

Domagaya, one of the Indians Cartier took to France, 54, 60; tells Cartier cure for scurvy, 87-8; taken to France again, 91; baptized at St Malo, 93; dies in France, 97.
Donnacona, Indian chief, called by Cartier Lord of Canada, 55, 59, 60, 65, 79; brings strange Indians to Stadacona, 89; taken to France by Cartier, 91; baptized at St Malo, 93; dies in France, 97.

East Cape, named Cape St Louis by Cartier, 37.

Francis I, 11; Cartier takes possession of land in his name at Gaspé, 34; and at Stadacona, 90; meets Donnacona and other Indians, 93; decides to assume sovereignty of New Land, 94; sends out Roberval expedition, 94, 95.
Funk Island, Cartier's Island of Birds, 15.

Gaspé Bay, wooden cross planted by Cartier at, 34-5.
Guyot, Charles, servant to Cartier, 89.

Hakluyt, translator of Cartier's narrative, 71, 103, 106.

Hochelaga, largest Indian settlement, 54; reached by Cartier, 69; Cartier again journeys to, 101.
Huron-Iroquois settlement at Quebec, 53.

Isle-aux-Coudres, named by Cartier, 51.

Jalobert, Mace, brother-in-law of Cartier, with him in second and third voyages, 43, 99.

Limoilou, Cartier's country place near St Malo, 110.
L'Isle au Massacre, 81.

Magdalen Islands, 25.
Miramichi Bay, 30.
Miscou, Point, first called Cape of Good Hope, 30.
Mount Royal, 69, 73, 76.

Newfoundland, fishing on the Banks, 8, 106; Cartier reaches, 12, 22; Roberval reaches, 106.
Nouel, Etienne, nephew of Cartier, 99.

Orleans, island of, first called by Cartier Isle of Bacchus, 52.
Ottawa river, described by Indians to Cartier, 77.

Pillage Bay, called a goodly gulf by Cartier, 46.
Pommeraye, Charles de la, with Cartier, 43.
Pont Briand, Claude de, with Cartier, 43, 69.
Port Daniel, 30.

INDEX

Prince Edward Island, supposed by Cartier to be mainland, 27.

Redclyffe, Cartier builds fort at, 99.
'Red Indians' of Newfoundland, 21.
Roberval, Jean François de la Roque, Sieur de, first viceroy and lieutenant-general of Canada, etc., 94, 105; meets Cartier at Newfoundland, 106; reaches Charlesbourg Royal, 108; attempt to explore the Saguenay, 109.

Saguenay, 46; Cartier first hears the name, 48; Cartier reaches mouth of, 50; massacre of Donnacona's people at, 80, 81.
St Catherine's Haven, named by Cartier, 13.
St Catherine, island of, 17.
Ste Geneviève, Mount, 46.
St Lawrence, Cartier ascends, 49, 50, 51.

St Lunario, Bay of, 29.
St Peter, Lake, first seen by Cartier, 67, 68.
St Malo, 1; birthplace of Cartier, 5; history of, 5, 6; Cartier sails from, 12, 42, 44; Cartier returns to, 92; Indians baptized at, 93; Cartier leaves on third expedition, 97; Cartier dies at, 111.
Scurvy, outbreak in Cartier's camp at Stadacona, 85-87.
Seven Islands, called by Cartier Round Islands, 48.
Stadacona, an Indian town, Cartier visits, 54, 78, 80, 97; mode of life of the natives, 82; their use of tobacco, 83.

Taignoagny, taken by Cartier to France, 54, 57-61, 63, 64; again taken to France, 91; baptized at St Malo, 93; dies in France, 97.
Toudamani, Indian foes of Donnacona's tribe, 80.
Tutonaguy, an Indian village, 102.

Printed by T. and A. Constable, Printers to His Majesty
at the Edinburgh University Press

1772600R0008

Printed in Great Britain
by Amazon.co.uk, Ltd.,
Marston Gate.